Marge and Gene Padgitt

Wood-Fired

Heating and Cooking

Wood-Fired Heating and Cooking
How to choose, maintain, and operate a
wood-fired appliance

By Gene and Marge Padgitt

ISBN 978-1-7378922-2-9

All photos copyright M. Padgitt or E. Padgitt unless otherwise noted.
Some photos by Adobestock.com
Cover photo: Adobestock.com

Printed in the USA

A Wood-Fired Publication

Published by HearthMasters Publishing
a division of HearthMasters, Inc.

PO Box 1166
Independence, MO 64051
Email: hearthmasters.office@gmail.com

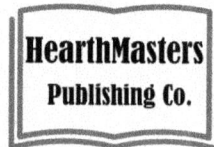

Marge and Gene Padgitt

"Fire is the most tolerable third party."

Henry David Thoreau

Acknowledgements

Thank you to Jesssica Steinhauser for providing information about her Kachelöfen business and to her husband, Dean Palmer for providing photographs.

Thank you to Alan Daugherty
for the Charcoal Selfie article and photos.

Thank you to Alice Brink for her Health Benefits of Fire in the Hearth article.

Thank you to Audrey Elder for her Chopping Therapy article.

Thank you to Andrew Truran for his DIY Plant Pot Tandoor Oven article.

Special thanks to the Chimney Safety Institute of America, the National Chimney Sweep Guild, the National Fireplace Institute of America, the Masonry Heater Association of North America and the many individual instructors for these organizations for providing classes and workshops over many years, which were invaluable to us.

Table of Contents

Table of Contents

Introduction

When Gene started our business in 1982 he had a good work ethic, the desire to learn, and a chimney sweeping kit with an instruction manual he purchased from August West. He soon found out that there was much more to the business, and a lot more he needed to know. I came on board full time in 1986 and we soon began to attend meetings and conventions and learn the real nuts and bolts of the chimney and fireplace business and how all of the different types of appliances work. Now we are sharing our knowledge with the public.

Everyone, no matter if they live in the country or city, should have an alternative heating and cooking method available at all times. Just go through one ice storm and have no electricity to run a fan on a gas furnace and you'll know the importance of being prepared. All of us who have experienced this know just how desperate a person can get if they are put in that situation. Using a kerosene heater is not a good idea as toxic fumes can overcome anyone in the house. And operating a gas generator to run a fan is also difficult when you must go outside to re-fill it with gas on a constant basis. For these reasons and more, the best emergency or alternative heating and cooking method is a wood-burning appliance.

Our company has had many experiences with homeowners who call right after their electricity goes out and expect us to not only have wood-burning stoves and inserts on hand, but be able to install them, along with a chimney, immediately. It doesn't work that way. Measurements need to be taken, an inspection completed, and the stove and chimney pipe or liner ordered before the installation of that type of appliance can happen. Not to mention that no one is getting on a snow or ice-covered roof in freezing weather to do the installation.

From the time a decision is made until the appliance and chimney are installed it will likely take at least two to four weeks. The best time to plan for heating is in the spring or summer, before you need it.

For the off-grid homesteaders and self-sufficient household a wood-heating appliance will likely be the primary heat source, and this book will help in the planning process. A wood-burning appliance is the only heating method that can be used independently of any other source, and it can be done efficiently with little emissions.

Wood is a renewable resource so it is by definition "Green." If trees are grown sustainably, there is nearly zero contribution to global warming.

In this book, we explain what each of the alternative heating and cooking methods are, how to purchase them, how to maintain them, how to choose and store wood for fuel, and what you need to know about chimneys needed for each type of appliance. And as a bonus, you'll find some of our favorite recipes in the back of the book.

We hope you find this book useful.

Chapter 1

Wood-Fired Heating

Welcome to the wonderful and magical world of wood-fired heating, where you will find that by using the energy stored in wood a home can not only be comfortably heated, but the benefits of radiant heat can soothe tired muscles and provide a relaxing atmosphere for you and your family.

Heating with wood is eco-friendly. Burning wood releases the same amount of carbon dioxide which would be released if the wood decayed on the forest floor. By burning it in an efficient appliance a home can be heated.

Anyone who wants to reduce their carbon footprint, enjoy passive heating, or have an alternative heating source should consider heating with a wood-burning appliance.

In this chapter the following are covered:

- Fireplace Inserts
- Freestanding Stoves
- Rumford Fireplaces
- Circulating Fireplaces
- Rocket Mass Stoves/Heaters
- Masonry Heaters/ovens
- Improving an Existing Fireplace
- The Wood-burning Furnace

The reader will note that pellet stoves, and wood-burning furnaces are not included in this book This is because they require electricity to work, and therefore, are not a reliable alternative heating method. They are, however, inexpensive appliances to use for heating a home so we consider them to be a standard heating method.

Standard open fireplaces are also not included because these types of fireplaces actually take heat from the home and they are not a heating appliance. Fireplaces are listed as "Decorative Appliances." Open fireplaces pull a lot of air from the house it is in, taking your nice warmed air from the house, which makes the rooms furthest away from the fireplace much colder. We do cover methods to upgrade or improve a regular open fireplace in this book.

Using and prepping the right type of wood is critical to the performance of any wood-fired appliance, so please be sure to read that section.

And finally, proper maintenance and care is crucial. All wood creates creosote, which is not only a fire hazard, but it can build up and prevent the appliance from drafting properly. There is work and maintenance involved when using wood-fired appliances. But the rewards are worth the effort.

A word about gas...

The reader may be considering a gas-fired insert or freestanding stove as well. If the desire is for low maintenance and no need for chopping wood, this is a good alternative. Just keep in mind that gas appliances produce approximately 50% of the heat that a wood-fired appliance produces.

Direct-vent gas appliances do need annual maintenance and tune-up by a professional gas service technician in order to maintain the warranty

The chart at the right shows the difference between each of the options for using a fireplace or a heating appliance. All types are included for comparison. Note that wood-burning stoves, fireplace inserts, furnaces, and masonry heaters produce the most heat. The costs for different types of fuel is included at the bottom of the chart. As you can see, wood is the least expensive fuel available, and if you have access to free firewood on your property, that is a bonus as the only cost is your labor.

Heating Appliance Comparison

Appliance	Efficiency	Price	BTUs (average)	Benefits	Disadvantages
Open wood or gas burning fireplace	0% Most of the heat goes up the chim-ney	$$$$	25,000	Ambiance	Can cool off the house Not for heating purposes
Electric logs or insert	98%	$	5,000	Ambiance	Not a heater
Open Rumford style or Bellfires wood or gas burning fireplace	40%	$$$	30,000+	Ambiance and heat, emergency heating	Must have wood availa-ble
Gas Direct Vent fireplace or Insert	76% - 89%	$$$	40,000	Ambiance and heat, emergency heating, remote control	Must have gas available
*Wood-Burning Insert or Stove	75% - 84%	$$$	80,000+	Ambiance, heat, emergency heating	Must have wood availa-ble
*Masonry Heater (Specialty site-built masonry appli-ance by a heater mason)	75% - 85% Uses small amount of wood	$$$$	80,000+	Ambiance, heat, emergency heating uses less wood than any other appliance	Must have wood availa-ble (but less of it)
Vent-free gas logs (we do not carry)	99%	$$	varies	Easy to use	Mold, bad odors, must use with open window
Pellet stoves or inserts (we do not carry)	80%	$$$	varies	Efficient source of heat	Pellets not always availa-ble. Must have electricity to use
Wood-Burning Furnace (Some can work in conjunction with gas furnaces)	60%– 85%	$$$	80,000-200,000	Cheap source of heat especially if wood is free or cheap	Must add wood several times a day. Uses a lot of wood.

US Forest Service Fuel Calculator		Annual Cost
Natural Gas	$7/1000 ft³	$854
Propane	$1.25/gal	$1,730
Seasoned Firewood	$115 /cord	$747
Electricity	.08/kWh	$2,390
Premium wood pellets	$120/ton	$882

and assure proper performance, so they are not maintenance-free. During this service the technician will clean the orifices, logs, and glass, check to see if the components are functioning properly, make certain the logs are placed properly, check the vent system, and do a test burn and CO test. If after reading this book you decided to go with gas (and we don't think you will) please don't forget to have the annual service completed.

Gas logs also need to be checked by a professional periodically. Most issues with gas appliances are because people don't have proper maintenance done.

And now on with wood…

What does it cost?

The cost of burning with wood includes a number of factors including whether you are purchasing cordwood, pallet wood, or chopping wood yourself. So the fuel cost could be $0 or up to the market price of a local cord of wood, which varies greatly across the United States.

Here are the current average prices for firewood:

A cord of hardwood in 2021 (Oak or Maple) runs between $250 - $450 per cord. Hickory is much higher. Mesquite can be found as low as $300 per cord.

A cord of softwood such as pine or juniper should cost between $200 - $250 per cord.

A cord of mixed wood should cost around $325 per cord.

Softwoods burn faster so you'll need more of it than if you use all hardwood.

The cost for delivery varies greatly from free to $100, and some firewood companies offer stacking services as well for an extra fee. You can usually specify the length of the logs to fit your appliance, which we recommend.

We use cordwood and also use pallet wood from a local contractor who gets large deliveries on heavy pallets made with 4" x 4" untreated wood. They cut it in to small pieces and stack them on pallets. We pick these up and can move the entire pallet with our pallet jack. These are very cheap - we pay about $45 per pallet for oak or yellow pine, which is very dense.

If you must use Hedge (Osage orange), use only one piece per load of wood. Hedge burns very hot and very fast, and is not only a fire hazard but can warp wood stoves in a short period of time, making them unsafe to use.

Note: Only burn cordwood or untreated pallet wood in any wood-burning appliance.

If you are lucky enough to live on some acreage and have trees on your property, the wood will be free, of course. There is another way to obtain free cordwood though. Check with your state forestry service. Most will allow you to take two or three cords a year of dead trees out of the forest for personal use. Just be sure it is local, and don't move firewood around to different regions.

See the section on choosing and prepping firewood for more information.

How wood burns

There is a science to how wood burns and produces heat. First, moisture is removed from the wood in the form of steam. Dark grey or black smoke is produced at this stage and this is when the most toxic gasses are produced. This is why you don't get much heat at startup and it is important to use dry wood, at 20% or less moisture content. After the water has been boiled off, the wood dries out and begins to burn the gasses coming off of the wood. When the smoke is all gone, glowing coals remain.

If there is not enough oxygen the fire burns slowly and may extinguish. Too much oxygen, and a wasteful roaring fire will result which will eat up the wood in no time. The object is to obtain the perfect balance between air and flame.

All fuels including gas, coal, wood, oil and propane produce CO_2. Responsible wood-burners will do everything they can to reduce emissions,

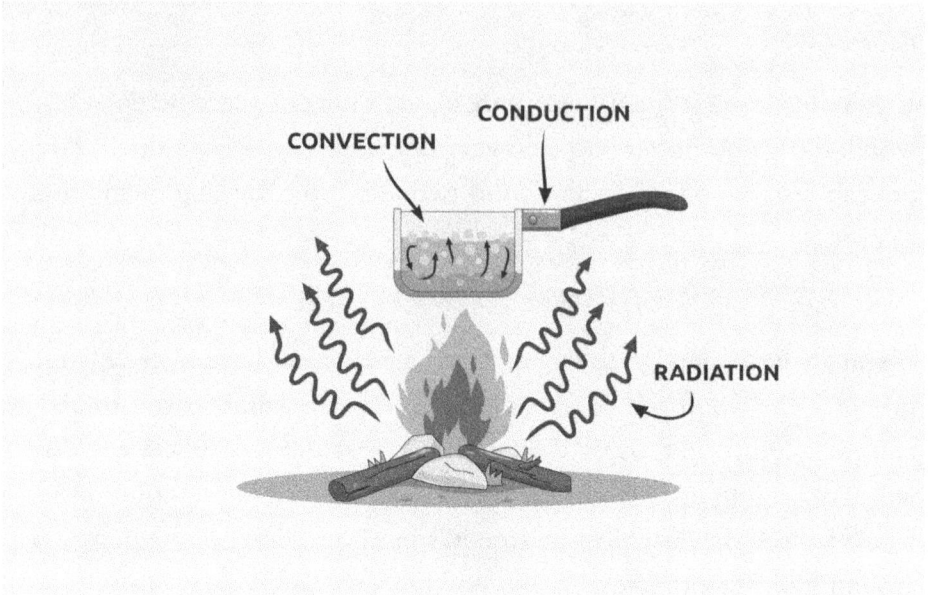

and that means using tested methods to burn efficiently. Burning efficiently means using less fuel as well.

How heat is distributed

Heat goes into cold through convection, radiation, and conduction. Convection is the transfer of heat by movement. Heat rises, so the upper levels of a home, or the ceiling will be warmer than the rest of the area. Convection is not the most optimal distribution of heat.

Radiation is the direct transfer of heat in the form of light (i.e.from the sun or a lightbulb). This light is often invisible to us, but it is there nonetheless. **Radiation** moves in straight lines in all directions and when it reaches a solid such as a couch or your skin it reflects and absorbs the heat. The drawback with this type of heating, however, is that the temperature decreases the further away you are from the source. In a small cabin this is not so much an issue, but in a house it can be a problem if there is no means to distribute the heat. Fans can alleviate this to a certain degree.

Conduction is heat by contact. Heat flows equally in all directions if the objects and air are the same temperature, but if not, heat goes into cold, so it seeks out cold first.

Thermal Conductivity Chart

Material	Density lb/in3	Thermal Conductivity Btu/(hr.ft.F
Brick	.069	.416
Glass	.093	.540
Cast Iron	.281	27.7
Steel	.283	26.2
Firebrick	.086	.65
Granite	.088	1.7-4.0
Limestone	.085	1.26-1.33
Porcelain tile	.083	1.5
Soapstone	.087	6.4

Sources:
https://www.engineeringtoolbox.com/thermal-conductivity-metals-d_858.html
https://www.theworldmaterial.com/density-of-metals/
https://www.tulikivi.com/en/tulikivi/Properties_of_soapstone

Different types of materials conduct heat at differing rates. Masonry materials such as granite are very dense so they conduct heat rapidly, while limestone and brick are less dense so they conduct heat more slowly. Metals, such as iron, conduct heat very quickly.

The point we are making is that the choice of appliance and the materials used is extremely important, and can make the difference in the final result, which is to heat your home efficiently and comfortably.

STEP 1:
Choosing the Right Appliance

The first step in this process is choosing the appliance that will work best in your situation. A professional chimney sweep or hearth installer should be consulted because they will be able to offer expert advise for your particular home. He or she will know the codes and clearance requirements and proper installation methods. This is not a DIY project.

In most jurisdictions, a Level 2 internal camera inspection per the NFPA 211 Standard is required when a masonry chimney is involved, or a site visit is required when installing a freestanding appliance or new appliance and chimney.

The following are some guidelines to use in the selection process:

Option A— Wood-Burning Insert

Alterra High-efficiency wood-burning insert by Regency

A good option is to utilize an existing masonry chimney and fireplace and install a wood-burning fireplace insert and stainless steel flue liner. See the following pages for a diagram of a masonry chimney, and a masonry chimney with a wood-burning insert installed. The new high-efficiency inserts are much more clean burning and use less wood than older model inserts. A stainless steel flue liner is installed inside the existing clay tile flue liner and in most cases the tile liner does not need to be removed. In the case of a stove that requires a larger flue liner the tile liner may need to be removed in order to make room for a properly sized liner. Older stoves typically have an 8" diameter take-off, or a rectangular or oval take-off where the flue liner is attached. A custom-made cast-iron boot will need to be made for older stoves with a transition piece to the round flue liner. This is something a professional must do.

Beware of Slammer Inserts!

Below: This 1980's model stove insert was pulled to clean the chimney. Note that there is a rectangular opening at the top and no steel flue liner is attached. This is an extreme fire hazard and not code compliant. Creosote accumulates on the smoke chamber and flue walls in the form of glazed/baked on creosote which is highly flammable.

Note: Much of our repair work on chimneys is due to installations like these. Avoid this type of installation.

Woodburning fireplace inserts should only be installed in MASONRY (brick or stone) chimneys. It is too risky to install an insert in a manufactured or prefabricated fireplace. This is not acceptable to code or the manufacturer. The UL listing of a manufactured fireplace is voided if a wood - burning insert is installed.

Slammer inserts are the cause of many chimney fires

9

**Diagram
of a masonry
chimney with
an open
fireplace**

Most of the heat
goes up the
chimney

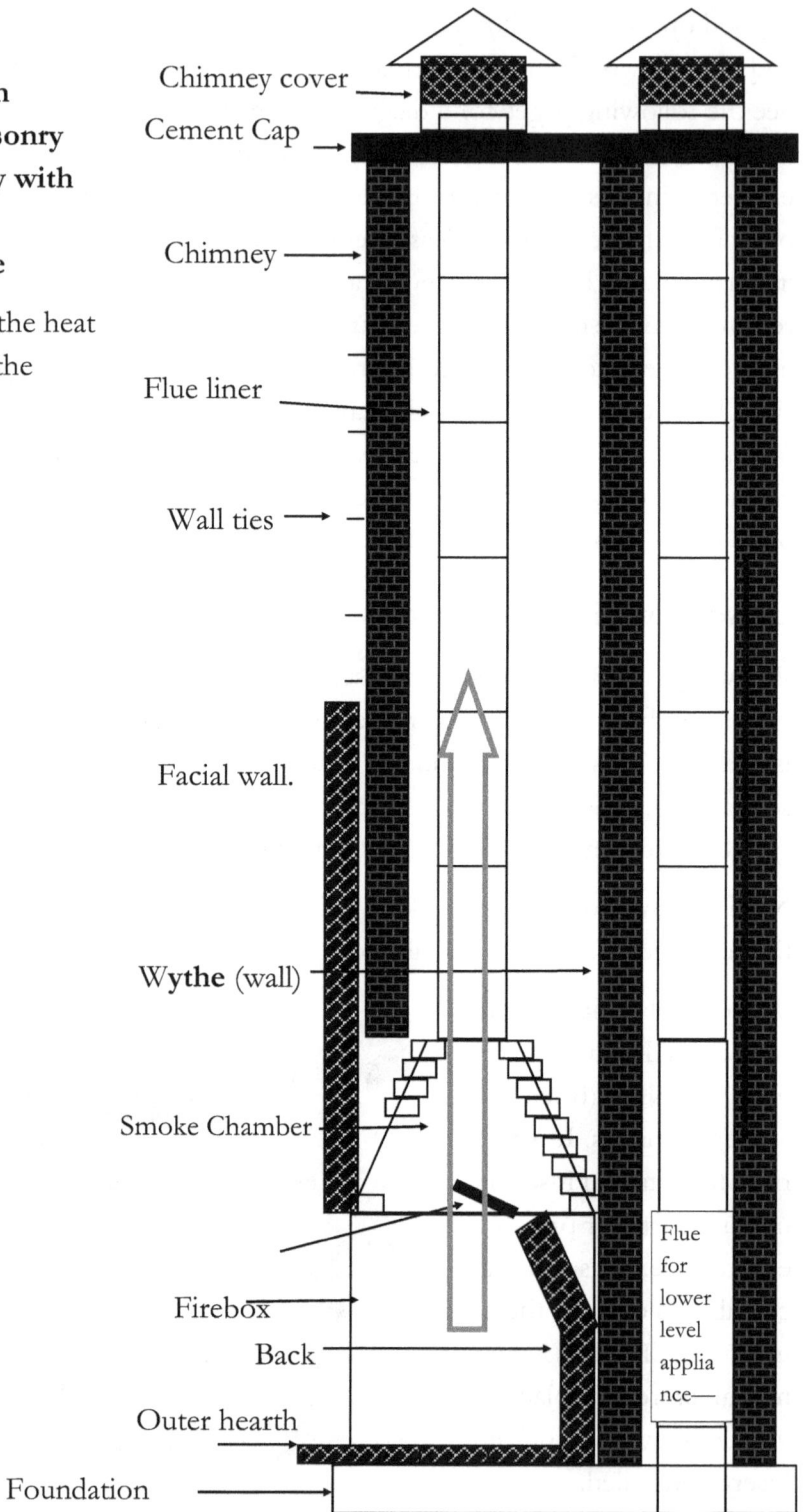

Chimney cover

Cement Cap

Chimney

Flue liner

Wall ties

Facial wall.

Wythe (wall)

Smoke Chamber

Firebox

Back

Outer hearth

Foundation

Flue
for
lower
level
applia
nce—

10

Installation of a wood burning stove insert into a fireplace:

The flue outlet is usually 6" - 8" in diameter or may be an oval shape. The required new stainless steel flue liner size will usually measure 5.5" - 6" on newer models.

The flue liner should be installed on top of the stove all the way to the top of the chimney. A top plate will be installed on top of the flue tile. The base is attached with a flue connector provided by the manufacturer or a custom-made "boot" can be made to fit on older models .

Proper installation of a woodburning insert includes checking for clearance to combustibles to mantels, wood trim, surrounds, and adequate hearth, and making sure flammable creosote is removed from the flue and smoke chamber before installation of the stove.

All new model inserts require this type of installation.

If you have an older woodburning stove you should notice less creosote accumulation and better performance of the stove after a new, properly sized flue liner is installed.

Burn fires hot. Smoldering fires are inefficient, produce more Carbon Monoxide, cause more creosote accumulation on flue walls, and don't allow a wood-burning stove to work properly. Wood stoves should be kept at 400-600 degrees. 700 and above is too hot and is not necessary. Watch the temperature of a wood stove because creosote ignites at 1,000 degrees without flame.

Tip:

Fireplace smoke chambers and flue liners are designed for open fireplaces only. They are too large for a stove insert to function properly, and are the cause of excessive creosote accumulation and chimney fires. This is why a smaller, properly sized stainless steel flue liner is required for use with an insert.

Diagram of a wood-burning insert installed in a masonry fireplace. This is the correct method of installation.

U.L. listed stainless steel flue liner installed from stove connector to top of chimney.

Wood-burning insert

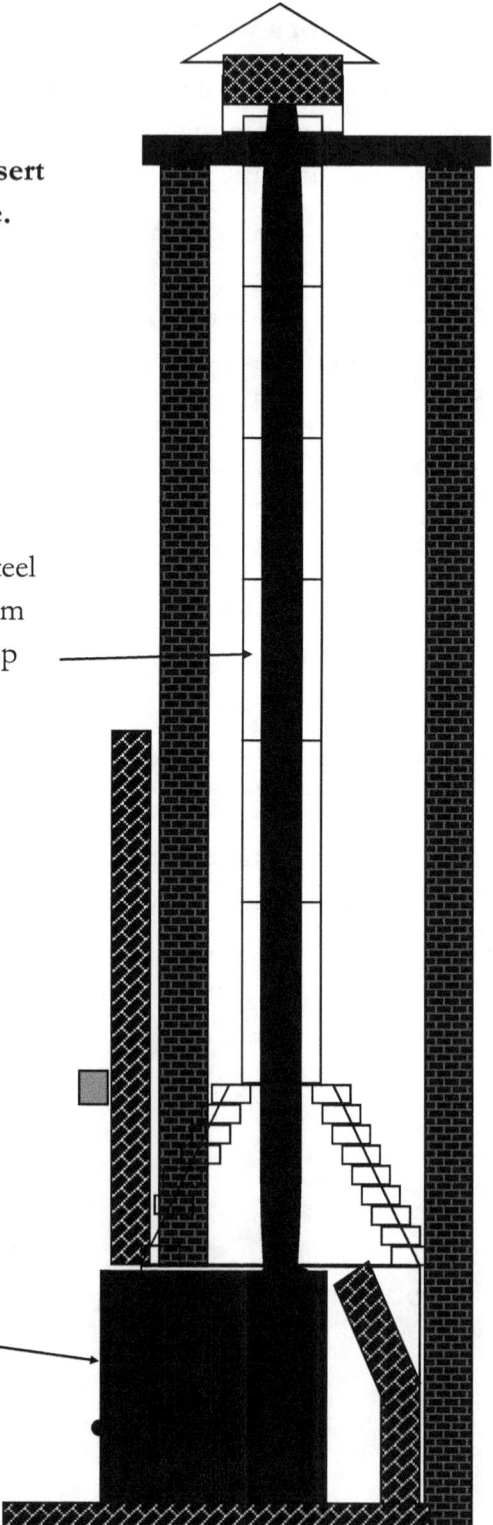

Diagram of a hearth stove utilizing an existing masonry chimney and fireplace.

This type of appliance is a cross between a freestanding stove and an insert. It utilizes the masonry chimney for venting. An advantage to this type of stove is that the top of it can be used for emergency cooking. However, it does take up a lot of room in front of the fireplace so for this reason is not a very popular option.

U.L. listed stainless steel flue liner installed from stove connector to the top of the chimney.

Hearth Stove

The hearth may need to be extended to comply with code (18") beyond the front.

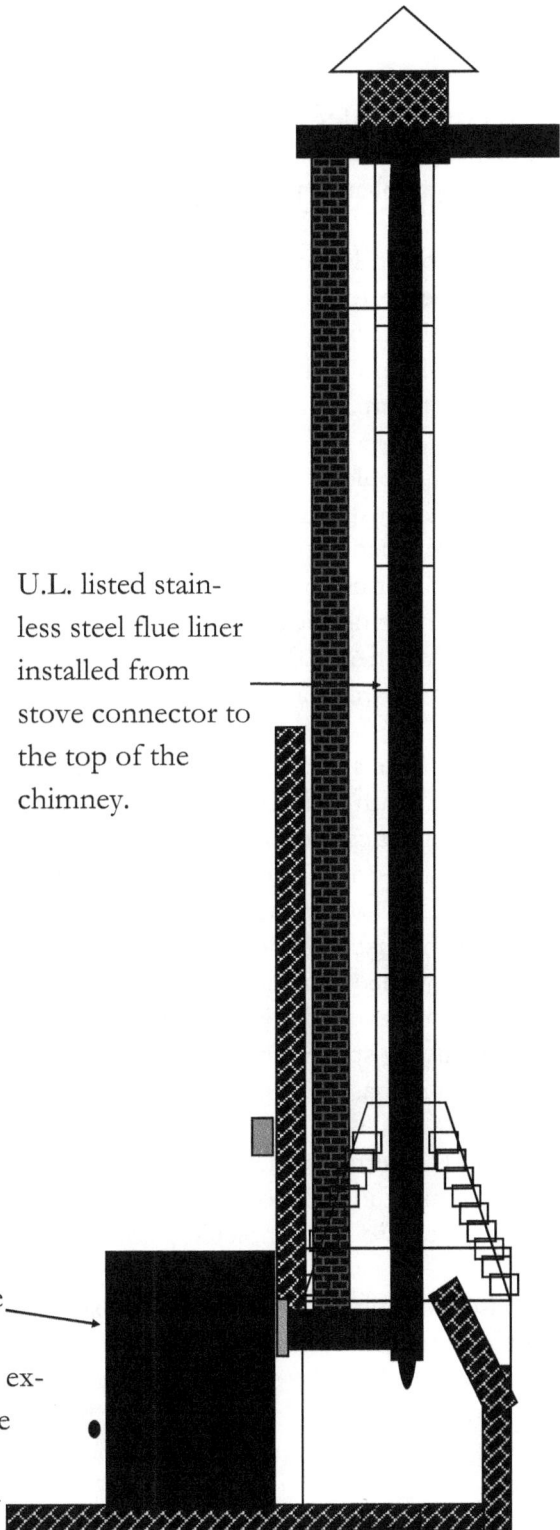

Wood-burning Inserts

If you've decided to install a wood-burning insert and know where the appliance will be located, there are more things to consider when choosing which appliance to purchase.

Most importantly, your professional installer should analyze the space that will be heated first. Factors involved are the size of the home, the layout of the rooms, the size of the room the insert will be placed in, how well the home is insulated, how high the ceilings are, and what the expectations are.

The insert should be sized properly in order to provide comfortable heating. The installer should tell the homeowner what they can expect as far as performance goes. It is not possible to go by manufacturer recommendations alone since the layout of the house is the most critical factor involved in sizing the appliance. For instance, if the manual states that the stove will heat 2,000 square feet, the actual result would be very different in a closed space verses an open concept living area.

The size of the stove should be at or larger than what is anticipated to be needed. With a larger stove, less wood can always be used but with a smaller appliance the firebox capacity will limit how much fuel can be placed in it at once. The firebox and brick facial wall surround may need to be modified or raised in order to accommodate the size insert desired, so the installer should be able to do this type of work. Newer model stove need smaller fireboxes to create the same amount of heat due to their design for efficiency. The key is not to overheat or under heat the living space. This is something that a professional will be able to determine based on a visit to the home.

A Level II internal camera inspection will be required prior to wood-burning insert installation by code. If repairs to the chimney are needed this will need to be completed prior to the installation of the insert.

All inserts require a properly sized (usually 5.5" or 6" for new models) stainless steel flue liner which is attached to the top of the stove and runs the length of the smoke chamber and flue. A top plate is installed along with a chimney cover to keep rain and animals out. This is not an option. The liner is required for proper draft and performance of the stove.

Many chimney professionals sell and install wood-burning inserts and flue liners so be sure to inquire about this before his/her visit to your home. Chimney sweeps are often the best installers of these types of appliances since they know the systems so well. Hearth Appliance dealers often employ chimney sweeps to do their installations if they don't have an installer on staff. Look for a Certified Chimney Sweep to do the installation. Someone installing for a hearth store should be a NFI (National Fireplace Institute) Certified Wood-Burning Specialist.

We do not suggest using a non-EPA certified wood-burning insert since in many states they are illegal to install. Instead, buy a brand new insert which is much cleaner-burning and uses less wood than older models to produce the same amount of heat.

Note: Check with your insurance agent before having any wood-burning appliance installed. They may require a certification by the installer.

Hearth Extensions

A Hearth extension may be required if the depth of the hearth is inadequate. This can be done using the same materials you currently have such as tile or bricks, or a hearth extension may be purchased from a hearth retailer or chimney sweep. These must be permanently affixed to the current hearth. Have a professional do this as they will know the clearance to combustible requirements underneath the hearth, and will be able to make any adjustments necessary.

Option B– Freestanding Wood Stove

Freestanding stoves are an option when there is no fireplace is present, or if you wish to add additional heat in a larger home. Many people have two appliances—an insert on the main level and a freestanding stove on the lower level or basement.

There are two ways to vent this type of stove.

Venting in a masonry chimney

Clay tile or a stainless flue liner: As previously mentioned, a freestanding stove may be vented into an existing masonry chimney that is designed for this purpose. A flue is installed, along with a thimble through the masonry, then black pipe is installed and connected to the top of the stove. In many cases, a vitreous clay tile flue liner is used, however, I suggest using a U.L. listed stainless steel flue liner instead. Stainless steel does not accumulate as much creosote and is easier to clean, making it less of a fire hazard.

Class A Chimney: A Class A chimney is required by all stove manufacturers when there is no masonry chimney available in the location where you wish to install the stove. Class A chimney pipe is double wall stainless steel with insulation between the walls. It comes in various sizes and lengths.

Poured Ceramic Flue Liner: This product is tested to U.L. 1777 for a zero clearance application, meaning that combustibles may be installed next to the chimney. So it is the best application to use if there are combustible materials installed that cannot be removed.

Don't use any other type of chimney because not only is it against code it would likely be a fire hazard.

NOTE: DO NOT USE BLACK PIPE AS A CHIMNEY! Black pipe is only allowed to be used for a connection from the stove to the chimney and is not designed as a chimney.

A modern freestanding wood stove. Photo: Adobestock.com

EPA Requirements for New Model Stoves 2020 and After

As of February 3, 2015 the Environmental Protection Agency required that all wood-burning appliances listed as heaters be certified to the US-EPA Phase II Standard for Emissions. All hearth retailers must carry only certified stoves. It is not legal to install an older, non EPA certified model. In 2020, the PM limit became more stringent.

PM (particulate matter): 2.5 grams per hour for catalytic and noncatalytic stoves tested with cordwood

PM is known as particle pollution and is a mixture of air-borne particles and liquid droplets composed of carbon, organic chemicals, metals, acid, and soil.

See the fact sheet here: https://www.epa.gov/residential-wood-heaters/fact-sheet-summary-requirements-woodstoves-and-pellet-stoves

This Waterford wood-burning stove heats the front part of our 2,500 sq. foot house: It produces 75,000 BTUs and has a stainless steel cooktop which came in very handy when we had a power outage.

A dragon steamer puts humidity in the air while a fan circulates heated air. The heat rising from the top of the stove turns the fan - no electricity needed.

A typical medium -sized stove such as this one will heat 1,100- 2,200 square feet of living space, depending on the layout of the home, ceiling height, and how well the house is insulated.

Notice the Chimfex chimney fire extinguisher on hand just in case of a chimney fire. And yes, even professional chimney sweeps have had chimney fires when they are too busy taking care of everyone else's chimneys instead of their own. Enough said.

Installation of a freestanding wood-burning stove with a Class A chimney through the roof

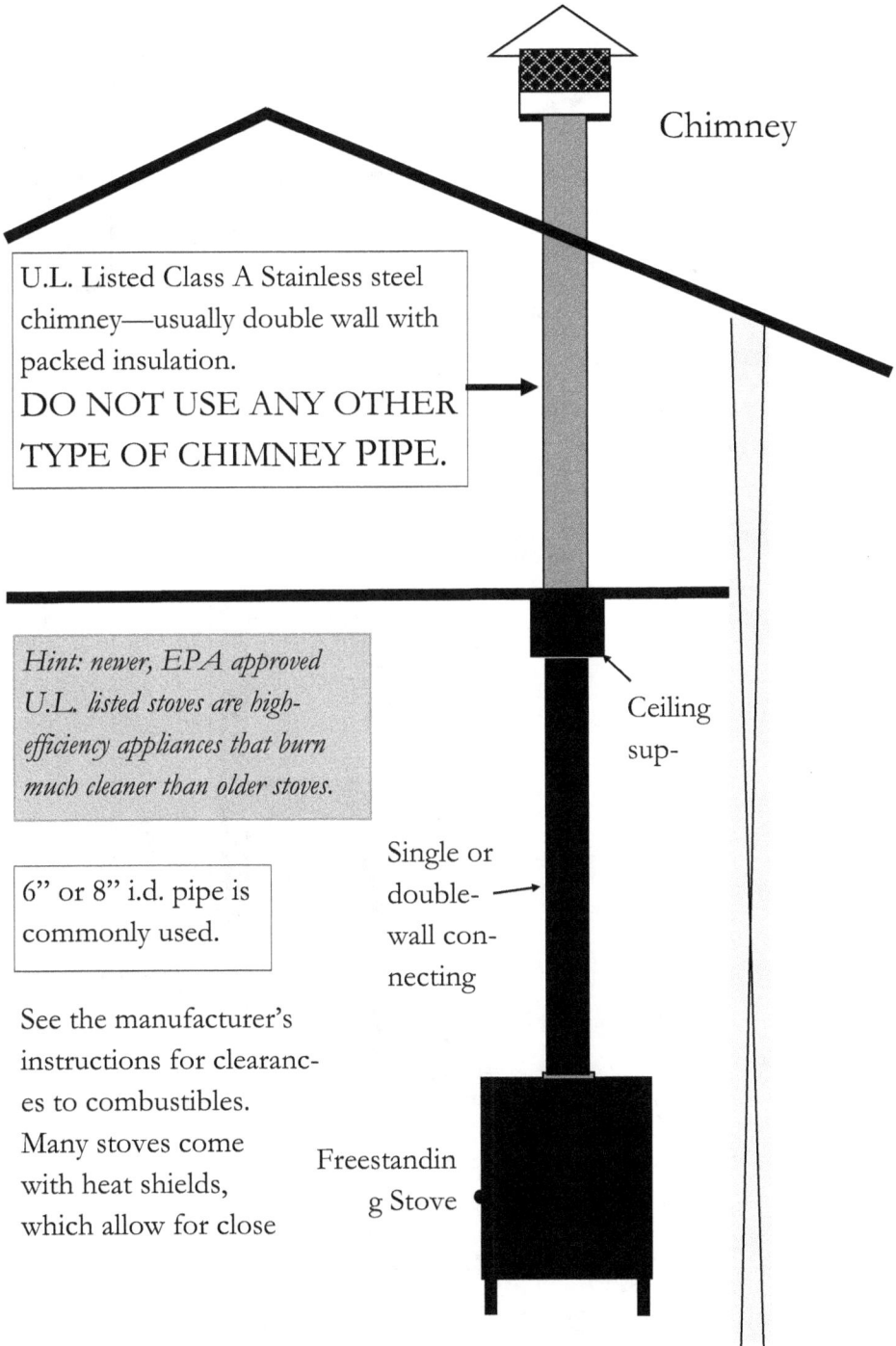

Chimney

U.L. Listed Class A Stainless steel chimney—usually double wall with packed insulation.
DO NOT USE ANY OTHER TYPE OF CHIMNEY PIPE.

Hint: newer, EPA approved U.L. listed stoves are high-efficiency appliances that burn much cleaner than older stoves.

Ceiling sup-

6" or 8" i.d. pipe is commonly used.

Single or double-wall con-necting

See the manufacturer's instructions for clearances to combustibles. Many stoves come with heat shields, which allow for close

Freestanding Stove

Installation of a freestanding wood-burning stove with a Class A chimney on the exterior

Chimney⟶
cap/

Installation of a freestanding wood-burning stove

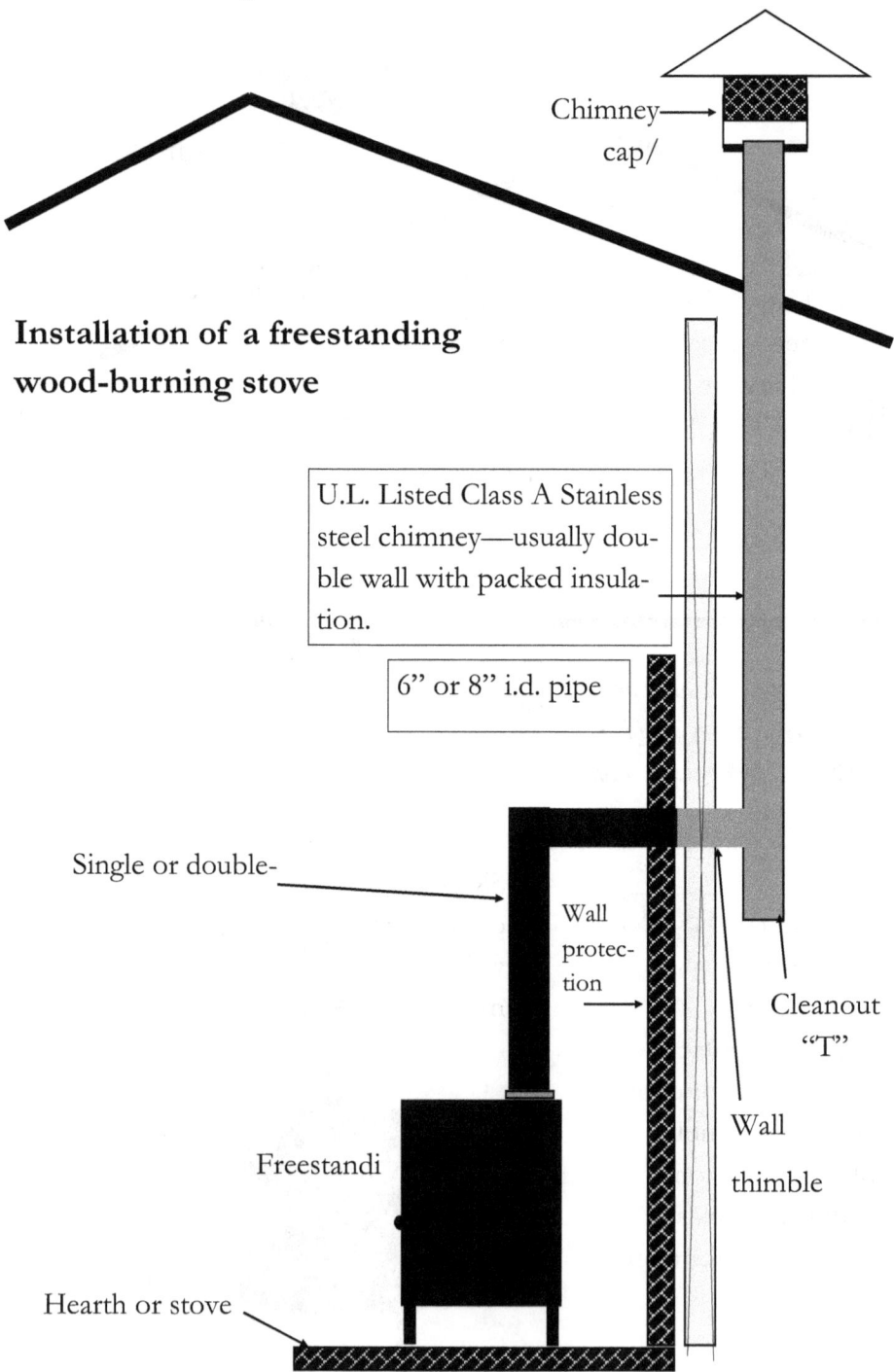

U.L. Listed Class A Stainless steel chimney—usually double wall with packed insulation.

6" or 8" i.d. pipe

Single or double-

Wall protection ⟶

Cleanout "T"

Wall thimble

Freestandi

Hearth or stove

Wood Stove Installation

If you've decided to install a wood-burning stove and know where the appliance will be located, there are more things to consider when choosing which stove to purchase. Most importantly, your professional installer should analyze the space that will be heated first. Factors involved are the size of the home, the size of the room the stove will be placed in, how well the home is insulated, how high the ceilings are, and what the expectations are from the homeowner.

The stove or insert should be sized properly in order to provide comfortable heating. The installer should tell the homeowner what they can expect as far as performance goes. It is not possible to go by manufacturer recommendations alone since the layout of the house is the most critical factor involved in sizing the appliance. For instance, if the manual states that the stove will heat X square feet, this would be very different in a closed space verses an open concept living area.

The size of the stove should be at or larger than what is anticipated to be needed. With a larger stove, less wood can always be used but with a smaller appliance the firebox capacity will limit how much fuel can be placed in it at once. The key is not to overheat or under heat the area. This is something that a professional will be able to determine based on a visit to the home.

An inspection will be required for wood stove installation in order to determine what floor and wall protection will be needed and the length of connector pipe and Class A chimney required. When purchasing a freestanding stove several components are needed: floor protection, wall protection (if closer to the wall location is desired), black single or double-wall connecting pipe, ceiling support kit, and Class A chimney with components. If planning to install a stove in a new home before construction, be sure to visit your chimney professional first and bring a set of home plans with you. Remember, the best location is in a central part of the home.

Tips:

- Reverse ceiling fans in winter to direct heated air downward.
- Review your expectations with your chimney professional before making a stove purchase.
- Purchase the stove from a reputable hearth dealer or chimney sweep.
- Check local building codes for permit requirements.
- Read the operation manual thoroughly and learn how to use the stove properly for optimal performance.
- Plan to have the chimney and connecting pipe swept out at least twice during the burning season to remove flammable creosote and improve performance of the stove.
- Don't expect the stove to do more than it was designed for.
- Add insulation to the attic or walls as needed to retain more heat.

The ECCO Stove

This stove is a really a hybrid stove/masonry heater that has been developed to achieve maximum efficiency by combining both conventional wood burning stove and slow heat release technology. It ha been in production in the U.K. since 2008. The Ecco Stove drives warmth through much more of the home without the need for plumbing, ducting, or electrical requirements using a Natural Heat method due to the patented Silicon Carbide (mineral/stone) body.

Some of the key features:

Slow heat release – Heat held in the stove body radiates for 7-12 hours after the fire has gone out.

One control – A simple mechanism makes getting the best out of your Ecco Stove easy.

Balanced heating – Won't over heat the room with hot and cold spots. Ecco Stove wraps the home in warmth with even heat distribution.

Low maintenance – Incredibly hard-wearing parts with 10-year warranty on the body.

High efficiency – Very low emissions passing the new 2022 Design standards for Europe.

Less re-fueling– From as little as two fires per day depending on home insulation levels and property size.

Safer environment – A much lower surface temperature than conventional wood burning stoves make the Ecco Stove much safer for children and pets to be around.

Clean environment – Carbon neutral efficiency helping the environment by only producing the same CO emissions as a tree decomposing naturally.

Made in the UK – Invented and manufactured in the UK

ECCO Stove by Landy Vent

the Ecco Stove is now exporting to
Belgium, Germany, France, Ireland, Italy, Canada, and the U.S..

UL Tested - Efficiency test, UL1482-10, Method 28A exemption test
and the Washington and Colorado parallel.

The advantage to this stove is that it is much lighter than a standard masonry heater, and can be installed fairly quickly. A Class A chimney system must be used with this stove/heater. It is shipped from the U.K. after an order is received from a dealer, so plan ahead.

Website: www.eccostove.com

Archguard carries a similar appliance called Salsburg XL Masonry Heater. It comes in three sizes in a linear design and produces 30,000 to 36,000 BTU's/hr. www.archgard.com

Option C—The Rumford Fireplace

Count Benjamin Thomas Rumford designed a fireplace in the 1700's that creates much more heat than a regular box style fireplace, so less heat is wasted up the chimney, and more heat is reflected into the room. Little has been done to improve on the design since.

A Rumford fireplace builder can build a new Rumford fireplace or "Rumfordize" an existing fireplace for you. Rumfordizing a fireplace is a solution to several problems, such as flues or smoke chambers that are too small to work properly, or for shallow depth fireplaces.

Count Rumford, for whom the Rumford fireplace is named, was born in Woburn, Massachusetts in 1753. He moved to Britain in 1776 during stressful war time. Rumford is known primarily for the work he did on the nature of heat. Back in England, Rumford applied his knowledge of heat to the improvement of industrial and residential fireplaces at the request of the Royal Family, who was concerned about the diminishing Black Forest. Rumford designed fireplaces that are shallower and narrower, with widely angled covings so they would radiate better. And he streamlined the throat, so as to "remove those local hindrances which forcibly prevent the smoke from following its natural tendency to go up the chimney..." Rumford wrote two essays

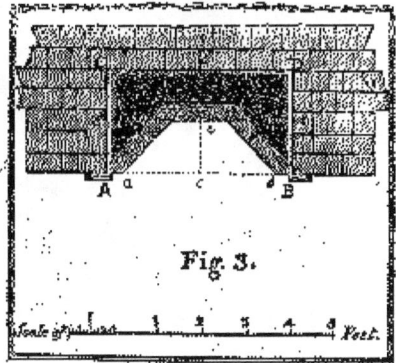

Drawings by Rumford

Left: This is a Rumford style fireplace under construction showing the back and side walls and inner hearth built out of firebrick and the damper installed on top.

Left: Continuing construction

Photos: Gene Padgitt, HearthMasters, Inc.

Rumfordizing: A method to modify existing fireplaces.

Rumford fireplaces have shallower depth, angled walls, smooth throat transition, and a smaller flue than is required for a box fireplace. It requires several modifications.

This style of fireplace is approximately 35—40% efficient.

Compare that to a regular box-style fireplace, which is ‾30% efficient to+10% efficient, and you can see the huge difference in heating potential.

Standard Fireplace VS Rumford Fireplace

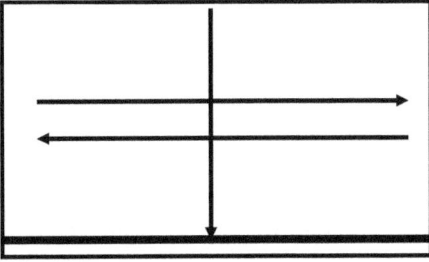

In a box style fireplace some heat is reflected into the room from the back wall, but is transferred back and forth on the inner walls.

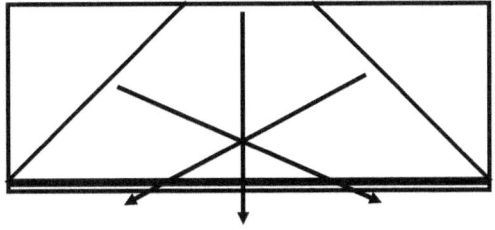

In a Rumford fireplace, the heat is reflected into the room from all three sides of the firebox, so more heat is produced.

Above: Gene headed up a Rumfordizing workshop for a non-profit organization in Oklahoma, and the team "Rumfordized" a 1930's box-style fireplace. The finished fireplace now heats the lodge. The side walls were removed and new side, back, and hearth floor were built using new firebrick. The smoke chamber was also modified. Note that the masonry is still damp right after completion of the project.

detailing his improvements on fireplaces in 1796 and in 1798. He was well known and widely read in his lifetime, an shortly after his modifications his "Rumford fireplace" became state of the art worldwide. The book *The Forgotten Art of Building a Good Fireplace* by Vrest Orton has detailed information on the Rumford design.

Rumford fireplaces were common from 1796, when Count Rumford first wrote about them, until about 1850. Jefferson had them built at Monticello, and Thoreau listed them among the modern conveniences that everyone took for granted. There are still many original Rumford fireplaces are often found buried behind newer renovations-throughout the country. Many are still in use in the U.K. and Europe. The Rumford is making a big comeback in the U.S. and other countries due to their efficiency.

A newer type of fireplace created using a modified Rumford design is a pre-cast fireplace and chamber system available through most Rumford masons. The one featured below is a *Bellfires* fireplace. It has a pre-cast floor, back, and side walls, and a stainless steel some dome. A Class A chimney is attached to the dome. Two styles are available - one for existing masonry fireplaces, and a close clearance fireplace which can be added to any room in the house. Visit www.bellfiresusa.com for more information on this product.

Above: This Rumford fireplace was built for a new construction project with a masonry chimney and stone face by Gene Padgitt with Hearth-Masters, Inc. The smoke chamber was made using a special form for Rumford chambers designed by Bob Hart. The stone is river stone sourced from a local stream by the homeowners. During an ice storm the owner's heat was out for two weeks, but they were able to stay in their home because this fireplace kept them cozy. Even we were surprised that it produced enough heat to keep the 3,500 sq. foot house warm.

Prior Fire Fireplaces

Chris Prior of Adirondack Chimney Company in Middle Grove, New York developed a modified Rumford fireplace that produces more heat than a standard Rumford.

Chris did testing on this for years, comparing different fireplace designs until he came up with the idea to modify the back wall. He and other masons built these by hand for years, but now HeatShield offers a pre-fabricated kit that is UL listed as zero clearance to combustibles with 4" nominal masonry. The kit has some improvements in design such as a secondary combustion feature which burns additional particulates before they reach the flue.

Note that the back wall juts out into the fireplace approximately 2/3 of the way up from the floor, then back. This feature directs heat back onto the fire, keeping it hotter and more efficient, producing more heat.

Below: A Prior Fire fireplace built out of firebrick by Gene Padgitt

Fabricated Rumford Style Kits

When some people hear the word "kit" they may believe that it is a DIY project, but this is not one of them. Leave this to the pros, and keep in mind that there aren't that many masons or chimney technicians doing this type of work so you may need to do some research to find a qualified installer.

This type of fireplace is manufactured masonry and made in to forms. The technician takes training from the manufacturer, then does the installation on site. Each fireplace is ordered in advance of the project, and there are several sizes available. There are three brands available: Ahren Fire, Bellfires, and Frisch/Rosin. The two most common are **Ahren (http://ahrenfire.com) and Bellfires (https://bellfiresusa.com**).

The kits are comprised of a stainless steel smoke dome, flue connector, and back, sides, and floor of the fireplace unit.

This type of fireplace is commonly used in older historic homes with small fireplaces that need to be replaced. The old fireplace is removed and the new unit with insulation and stainless steel flue liner is installed, then finish work completed on the face of the fireplace.

Bellfires also manufactures a zero clearance fireplace system with the smoke dome built in and ready to install in any location.

Superior Clay manufactures Rumford smoke chambers and fireplace throats out of clay. These are a good option when building a site-built Rumford fireplace out of firebrick. Visit **https:// www.superiorclay.com/fireplaces/rumford-fireboxes/rumford-components** for more information.

The newest addition to kits is the **PriorFire Retrofit Fireplace System** available at https://heatshieldchimney.com/priorfire/

Visit any of the manufacturer sites to see a list of qualified installers.

Bellfires Kit Installation

During installation: Stainless steel smoke dome and back and sidewalls installed.

A Bellfires installation during and after. The original fireplace surround and tile were reinstalled and a new marble outer hearth was installed.

Option D– Circulating Fireplaces and Fireplace Furnaces

For Serious Experienced Wood burners only

This type of fireplace furnace should be planned during the construction phase. It is difficult to add later. It must be encased in masonry construction with more stringent clearances than a standard fireplace, therefore, NFPA 211 Standards for regular chimney and fireplace construction do not apply to all aspects of this type of installation.

A professional mason who specializes in these types of fireplaces must do the construction and installation.

Circulating fireplaces produce heat by capturing heat in tubes, which open in vents above the fireplace. The air input is carefully managed to provide just the right amount of oxygen for the fire to burn hot, but not too hot. They do produce a good amount of heat, in some cases over 180,000 BTUs. Most of these units however, are not high-efficiency and they use up a lot of wood.

At first glance, this type of fireplace furnace may seem like a good idea, but as a company on the service side we can say that they are usually a problem for the homeowner.

Reasons not to use a circulating fireplace with tubes:

♦ Homeowners rarely have them maintained properly.

♦ The tubes above the damper make access to the flue impossible.

♦ There is rarely an outside access door installed so the flue can be swept and flammable creosote removed.

♦ These types of fireplaces are, unfortunately, the cause of many chimney fires because the flues simply cannot be swept properly.

Even if there are no tubes in the way and an access door—homeowners rarely have them maintained, which leads to chimney fires.

Heat circulates behind the fireplace and through tubes, then exits through the vents

This heat-circulating fireplace has a metal firebox and metal smoke dome. The masonry around it must be installed to the manufacturer requirements. After many years of use, the metal firebox and smoke dome may become warped and the seams could separate, making replacement of the entire unit necessary.

When replacement is necessary, this requires removal of the entire face wall and rebuilding after the new unit is installed.

Do not over fire any appliance, especially these types of heating appliances, where damage to the metal firebox is possible.

However, if you are an experienced wood burner, and feel confident that you can operate and maintain this type of fireplace furnace, and it has an access door in the back of the chimney for cleanout, by all means, go for it!

Twice yearly sweeping and inspection should be done by a professional chimney sweep. If there are no chimney sweeps in your area purchase a set of cleaning rods and brush that fits the flue and do it yourself. Put a reminder on your calendar so you don't forget.

Close-Clearance Fireplace Heater

This is a Regency brand P-90 Fireplace (The newer models are numbered differently). It produces 80,000 BTUs. The fireplace is installed in wood

and steel stud framing and uses a Class A stainless steel insulated chimney system. Heat exits through the vent above the firebox. Combustion air enters through the vent below the firebox. **These units are highly efficient and clean burning**, and use much less wood than a fireplace furnace.

Left: before finishing work was completed.

Option E– Masonry Heater

The Cadillac of Wood Heating

"Consider these aspects of the Masonry stove. One firing is enough for the day; the cost is next to nothing; the heat produced is the same all day, instead of too hot and too cold by turns; one may absorb himself in his business in peace. Its surface is not hot; you can put your hand on it anywhere and not get burnt, yet one is as comfortable in one part of the room as another."

Mark Twain
From "Some National
Stupidities" written in 1891

Masonry heaters have been around since Roman times in Europe, but are just recently catching on in the U.S. One of the great things about masonry heaters is that they are GREEN. Many years ago, people needed to heat their homes in an efficient manner just as today in order to save their forests. Inefficient open fireplaces took too much of their valuable resources, so another method had to be developed. No one knows who the first mason was who came up with the idea of devising something that would retain heat for long periods of time, then radiate it into the home while using much less wood, but whoever he (or she) was - they were a genius.

Masonry heaters have been redesigned and altered over the years by different masons in Finland, Russia, Germany, Austria, and the United States. But masonry heaters all have the same characteristics with complex channels to slow down and trap heat from flue gasses, and a mass of masonry to retain that heat, then radiate it to the living space over a period of up to 20 hours.

By the time the products of combustion get to the exit of the flue, the smoke is white or clear and the particulate emissions are very low. One load of wood can usually provide heating for the average size home for

8-12 hours. Compared to even the best high-efficiency wood–burning stoves on the market today, gas and oil-fired furnaces, and certainly inefficient open fireplaces, masonry heaters can't be beat. Homeowners may use a masonry heater as their sole source of heat, or in conjunction with another system.

Another benefit masonry heaters offer is that they don't require electricity, gas, or ductwork to distribute the heat. In a properly designed home with an open floor plan and the heater in the center of the home, the heat will radiate evenly throughout. Ideally, heaters are built in new home construction, but they can be added to existing homes if the layout is right. If planned in a passive solar home, the masonry mass of the

Custom-made brick masonry heater with an oven installed above the firebox.
By Gene Padgitt.

heater will also absorb and radiate heat from the sun as well. Heaters require a suitable foundation to support the massive masonry, which weighs three to six tons by the time all of the firebrick, block, cast iron doors, dampers, and exterior masonry facing is installed.

Heaters can be enhanced with heated benches to sit on, mantels, wood storage bins, and even bake ovens. Pizza and bread from a wood-fired bake oven has an incredible and unique taste that is not to be missed, but entire delicious meals can be cooked in the oven if desired. An experienced heater mason can not only design and build the right size and type of heater for a home, but make it beautiful to look at as well. An exterior finish of soapstone, tile, natural stone, stucco, or brick can make a dramatic statement. Heater masons will work with the homeowner to come up with a custom design that suits the home, or use one of many masonry heater kits that are available from several manufacturers

Finnish soapstone heater installed by HearthMasters crew with Gene Padgitt and Jerry Frisch. A bake oven is included on the kitchen side.

(usually incorporating soapstone) in a variety of designs.

Use of natural non-toxic materials and the renewable resource of wood make masonry heaters the perfect solution for any home.

The trade is very specialized, with only a few heater masons scattered across the U.S. Fortunately, most of these masons will travel to do installations. Some have even traveled to Japan, China, and South America to build heaters. Often several heater masons will help each other out since these are big projects. In days of old, the heater masons kept their trade secret, even to the point of locking themselves in a room for days until the heater was completely finished so no one else could see how the interior was completed. This assured them constant work. At that time, the livelihood of the masons was dependent on this secrecy. The trade is so skilled that the only way to learn is to do hands-on assistance with an experienced heater mason, and that is part of the reason the Masonry Heater Association was formed. The older masons do not want this to become a lost art, so they help train others. The Certified Heater Mason program was developed by the experienced MHA members in order to assure that the knowledge is not lost.

Pricing for heaters is what most would consider being on the high end, and a long-term investment. The average cost a homeowner may expect to pay is from $30,000 to $60,000, with price depending on the complexity of the heater, size, material costs, and labor. The expected time to get a return on your money is approximately 10 years. The time to build a completed heater may be more than four weeks, depending on how many skilled craftspeople are working. Many homeowners will elect to be an assistant on the job in order to lower their costs. In some cases, if a heater mason is traveling the homeowner will put him up at their house or a local hotel. When traveling the masons usually work long hours in order to get the project done sooner.

Find out more about masonry heaters, including technical specifications and testing results, photos of heaters, manufacturers, and a list of heater masons, contact the Masonry Heater Association of North America

Above: Granite masonry heater with bake oven. This heater is two-sided
and has doors on the opposite side for loading wood
[Join our group on Facebook: **Masonry Heater/Rocket heaters/
Kachelofen Hub**]

through their website at www.mha-net.org.

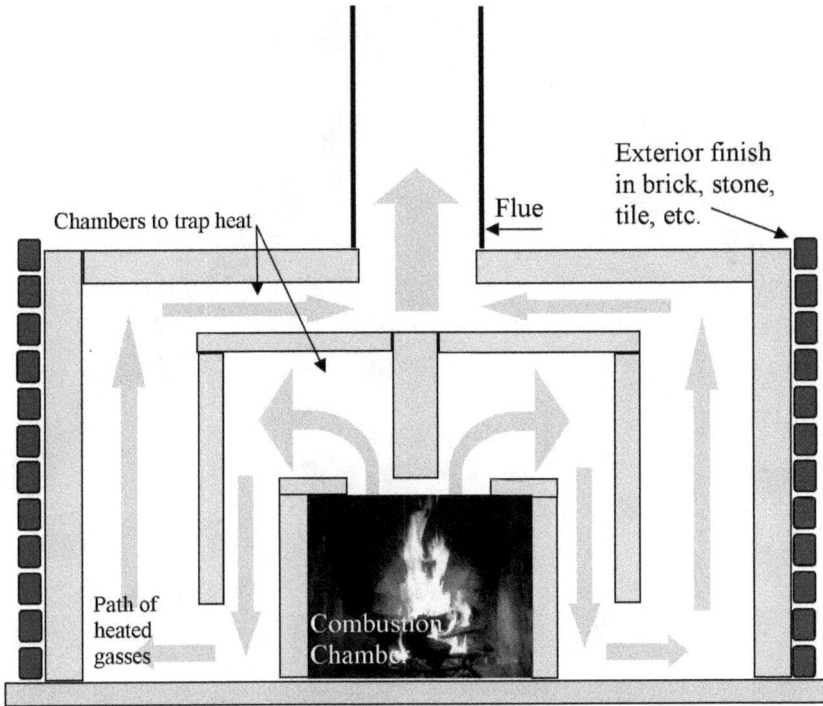

Chambers to trap heat

Flue

Exterior finish
in brick, stone,
tile, etc.

Path of
heated
gasses

Combustion
Chamber

Simple diagram of a Swedish contra flow heater

Interior of part of the heater from the top down during construction

This custom two-sided stone face masonry heater has a firebox opening in the back and front, and an oven on the kitchen side. This gourmet chef wanted only the best for her home. She wanted a more rustic look that the stone provided. Notice the clean out openings in the raised hearth. This is a *White Oven*, which utilizes heat from the firebox below. No wood is burned inside the oven. *Black Ovens* are so–called because wood is burned inside the oven.

Designed and built By Gene Padgitt Photos: HearthMasters, Inc.

The Kachelöfen

1500's Tile Stove in the Kirner Gallery section of the UBC Museum of Anthropolgy in Vancouver, CA. Leoboudv, CC BY-SA 3.0 <https://creativecommons.org/licenses/by-sa/3.

It is believed that tiled stoves likely originated in the Alps in the late 13th century. Open fireplaces were inefficient and used up a lot of precious wood, so there was a need for a more efficient appliance. The idea developed from a simple clay dome to an ornate tower-like structure with hidden channels inside to trap heat. Open fireplaces were often replaced with this appliance when the tiled stove became aesthetically pleasing and suitable for use in palaces, castles, convents and monasteries. The surfaces of the tiles were decorated with various scenes or designs.

The top level of the tiles on the stove at the left portray the Expulsion of Hagar (from the Old Testament), the second level of tiles portray musicians, the third level depicts the twelve apostles, and the tiles on the firebox are decorated with unidentified portraits. The Tiled stove dates to c.1560 and is made of lead-glazed earthenware. The builders often kept their craft secret. It originates from either Germany or Central Europe. Today there are a few artisans in the world who still create the tiled stove or Kachelöfen.

Left: Jan Długosz House in Sandomierz Sandomierz, Poland. Diocesan museum.

Credit: myself (User:Piotrus), CC BY-SA 3.0 <https://creativecommons.org/licenses/by-sa/3.0>, via Wikimedia Commons

Wood-Fired Heating and Cooking

The following was first published in the winter 2015 issue of Wood-Fired Magazine:

Jessica Steinhäuser is an award-winning Canadian ceramic artist, who is gaining international renown for her Kachelöfen – wood-burning ceramic heaters that marry ancient technology with contemporary art.

Jessica's Kachelöfen are in private collections around the world, including Three Glens, an ultra-modern, sustainable farmhouse in Scotland that won a Green Apple Environment Award in 2013. She has also been featured in The Telegraph, BBC Scotland, World Architecture News and other high profile media, as well as in The Globe & Mail, Ceramics Monthly, Dwell.com, Grand Magazine and other publications.

Jessica trained and apprenticed as a potter at Staatliche Fachschule für Gestaltung (State School for Art and Design) in Nürnberg, Germany in 1984-85. She then entered Staatliche Keramikfachschule (State School for Ceramics) in Landshut, Germany, where she earned her Graduate Journeyman Potter certification in 1988. She has also studied with kachelöfen builders in Austria (2004), and with master stone carver Nicholas Fairplay in Guelph.

The kachelofen building process begins when Jessica meets with the client to determine the size and style, then she puts pen to paper and draws a sketch. Next, Jessica begins construction by using her own clay mixture which is specially mixed with a lot of grog for stability.

Jessica said that "Kacheln are more like hollow bricks, not flat tiles. Kachel comes from the word cacabus in old high German which means "bowl or pot."

The time it takes to form the kacheln in a mold then dry completely before firing is approximately one week. Jessica sometimes weighs down the kacheln with square batts with bricks on top to keep their shape. Each kachel will shrink by 7% during the entire process, so the plan must include the shrinkage factor.

The firing time in the kiln for the first firing is 1060C (1940 F) for 10-12

Kachhelofen by Jessica Steinhauser   Photo: *Dean Palmer Photography, Guelph, Canada*

hours. The second firing is kept at 1050C (1922F) for 8 hours. After the kacheln are completed, they are shipped to the location and Jessica and her team assemble the project on site. It takes several days or to complete the project.

Kachelofen are not simple projects by any means. The process incorporates an interior firebox and channels to trap heat like standard masonry heaters. The similarity ends there. The finished exterior, made from custom-made kacheln (heavy ceramic tiles) makes for a beautiful finish. Not that stone and brick masonry heaters are beautiful, too, but this is a completely different look, and certainly one of this writer's favorites.

The technology has existed in different forms from ancient times. Archeological digs have revealed excavations of ancient inhabitants utilizing hot smoke from fires in subterranean dwellings. The heat would radiate into the living spaces and warm baths. These early forms of heaters evolved into modern-day systems. During the Roman Empire, Hypocausts were used in upper-class homes. A hypocaust was a system of underfloor heating used to heat houses and baths with hot air.

Wood-Fired Heating and Cooking

In Eastern and Northern Europe and North Asia, Kachelöfen or masonry stoves evolved in many different forms, with the building methods usually kept a very closely guarded secret among builders. There are Russian Stoves, Finnish Stoves, German Stoves, and Swedish Stoves, (known as contra-flow heaters).

Jessica is truly a unique artist, blending efficient old-world technology with ceramic artistry to create functional and beautiful heating appliances. Her website: **www.stonehousepottery.com**

Kacheln being laid out in Jessica's shop

Photo by Dean Palmer Photography, Guelph, Canada

Option F: Rocket Mass Heaters/Stoves

Rocket Mass Heaters were first developed for third world countries as an inexpensive way to heat and cook using readily available materials such as cob. These appliances are ever-evolving as people experiment with different designs. Unlike other types of heating appliances, there is no U.L. listing, and no manufactured firebox to purchase, and it *can* be a DIY project, although you may want to hire a pro for your first project.

Rocket stoves are very popular among self-sustaining communities, homesteaders, cob and straw bale home builders, and are now gaining interest among the general public. They are a good less expensive alternative to other types of wood-fired heating appliances if you don't mind getting dirty and doing some hard work to build one. Chose to build a stove, a heater, or a combination of the two, and add a heated bench for some added benefit.

There are also metal rocket stoves being built for outdoor use, and some are very small, yet get the job done. Basically, rocket stoves are small chimneys with an opening at the bottom for the wood and air intake. They can be built with cob, bricks, or metal - anything that is fire proof. Don't use aluminum or copper because these metals melt easily and will be gone in short order.

Rocket Heater Diagram

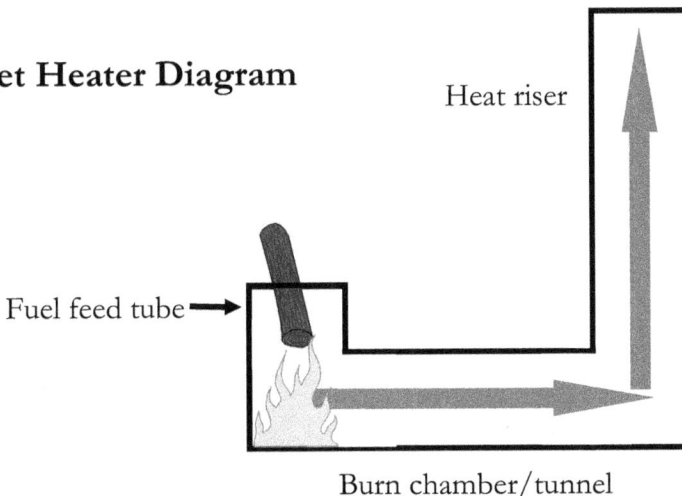

Heat riser

Fuel feed tube →

Burn chamber/tunnel

Rocket stoves/heaters work differently than other types of appliances, making them very unique. There are three components to a rocket stove:

1. A burn chamber with an opening at the top (instead of the standard side opening in other types of appliances)

2. A heat capturing tube that keeps heat inside the house.

3. A chimney.

All of these components create a stove that is entirely inside the house, so heat is kept inside the structure. The long tube section is covered with a non-combustible material (like cob) and can be used as a cozy bed or bench.

The only possible drawback is that the stove takes up floor room, but this is only a slight inconvenience compared to the benefits.

We do not build rocket stoves but have seen them being built at the Masonry Heater Association annual meeting, and know rocket stove builders, who swear by them. We highly suggest reading a few books on this subject before going forward with plans for a rocket heater. Visit www.rocketstoves.com for a list of books on the subject.

Try building a small rocket stove yourself to test out how it works. Plans are at the right:

To build a small outdoor rocket cook stove out of bricks:

Gather at least 24 bricks and lay them out in this pattern on a flat surface using full and half bricks:

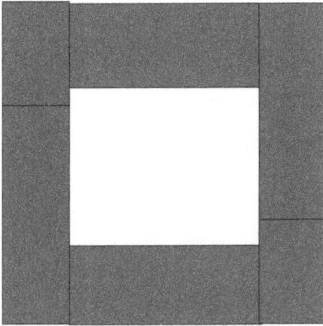

Second course

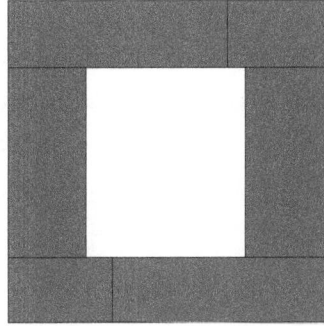

Third course

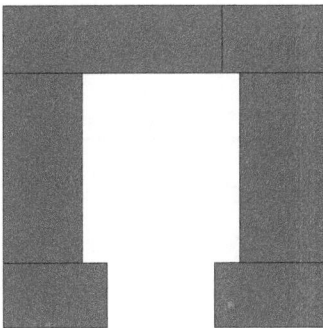

First course with opening for wood

Place a grate at the top and place your cookpot on top of that.

Repeat the second and third courses until the stove is finished. There is no need to use mortar unless you want to make it a perma-nent structure. Build away from the house.

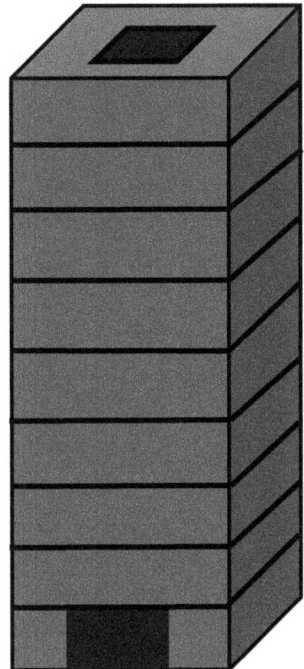

Rocket mass heaters use small pieces of wood rather than the large pieces most wood-burners are accustomed to, therefore, dead sticks from the yard will do nicely. The fuel is burned quickly, then the air intake is closed in a similar fashion to a masonry heater. And like a masonry heater, the heat is trapped inside via channels and the masonry is heated, then radiates heat into the room. These appliances are very clean-burning and produce little pollutants. Rocked mass heaters are usually designed around a stainless steel barrel with channels built inside to trap heat, but other materials can be used:

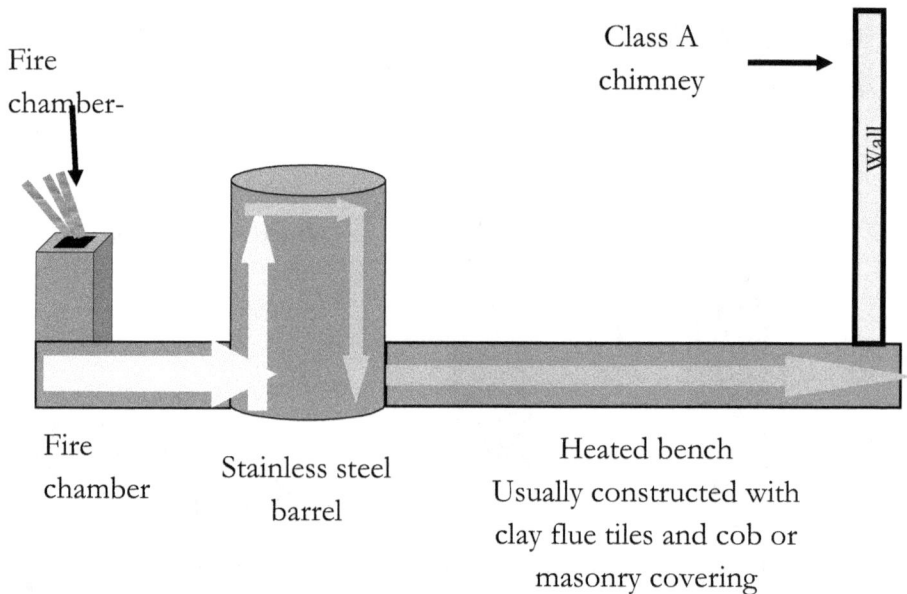

Fire
chamber-

Class A
chimney

Wall

Fire
chamber

Stainless steel
barrel

Heated bench
Usually constructed with
clay flue tiles and cob or
masonry covering

Diagram of a Rocket Mass Heater

(There are variations on this)

Also do a Google search and check out the Facebook groups on the subject.

Option G: Improving an Existing Fireplace

If you have no other option, take these steps to improve the efficiency of your existing standard box-style masonry fireplace:

Note: DO NOT use these methods on a manufactured fireplace since it would be a fire hazard. Manufactured fireplaces cannot be altered in any way or the listing and warranty will be voided.

1. Install a cast-iron or stainless steel fireback. This serves two purposes - to reflect heat into the room and to protect the back wall of the fireplace from logs that are thrown onto the grate. This method has been used for centuries and it really does work!

2. Circulating grates are available from Thermorite.com and other manufacturers. These are to be used in conjunction with Thermorite doors, which essentially seal off the fireplace and control the amount of air flow. The grate has tubes that circulate heat to the top and out the top portion of the glass doors, while the air inlet is located at the base of the doors. A fan moves the heated air. This needs to be connected to an electrical outlet. This system can be used with gas logs or wood. Thermorite's grate brand is Cozy Grate. Their website is www.thermo-rite.com. This type of set up is not inexpensive, however, you may be able to obtain a used grate from an auction site such as EBAY.

Option H: Wood-Burning Furnaces

There are two types of wood-burning furnaces - indoor and outdoor. While most of these types of appliances are purchased by farmers and country people , there are a few city dwellers who use them as well. The outdoor furnace is placed outside on a pad and wood is placed into the fire chamber from the outside of the house. This requires going outside in winter to re-fuel the chamber.

Indoor furnaces are often placed next to gas-fired furnaces and utilize the same ductwork to distribute heat throughout the home. Most operate independent of the homeowner (except for feeding it wood) so the gas furnace will kick on if the fire is allowed to go out when the homeowner is not around to refill the fire chamber. The advantage to this type of furnace is that it does not require a trip outside every time wood is needed.

Older furnace models are not efficient and burn "dirty." Newer models are considered to be high-efficiency and we recommend this type, not only because it is better for the environment but because less wood is needed to produce heat.

Wood-burning furnaces produce 150,000 - 200,000 BTU's, which is comparable to standard gas-fired forced air heaters, and is more than enough to heat the average size home.

Radiant in-floor heating, hot water systems, and snow and ice melting systems for driveways and walkways are available to use with some wood -burning furnaces.

Some efficient EPA phase 2 certified Wood-burning furnace manufacturers are WoodMaster (www.woodmaster.com), KUUMA (www.lamppakuuma.com), and HeatMaster (www.heatmasterss.com).

Chapter 2
Managing Your New Appliance

Installation Location

In an ideal situation, this decision would be made at the time plans are drawn up for a house, and the installer would be able to consult with the architect, builder, and homeowner. But in most cases, the appliance is installed after the house is built, so that limits where it can be placed.

A central location with an open floor plan is best so that heat can evenly radiate around the house.

But you many need to work with what you've got so even though it won't be ideal, you'll still get lots of heat!

An existing chimney, or location of a previous chimney may be able to be utilized. If this is possible, it will save you some money. But sometimes it will requires removal of the existing chimney and construction of a new one out of masonry, or a wood chase for a Class A chimney.

If the location is not ideal or not enough heat is produced to heat rooms that are further away, you may need to consider adding another heat source in that area.

Small woodstoves are popular in sunrooms and master bedrooms. Larger wood-burning appliances are best used in large family rooms or open concept areas because they produce a lot of heat.

Sizing is important because you want enough heat, but not too much or you'll be heated out of the room the appliance is located in. Wood-burning appliances vary in size and BTUs produced, varying from 45,000 to 120,000 BTUs.

Consider where the chimney will be located and if it is a practical spot. Keep Class A stainless steel chimneys to the rear of the house for aesthetic purposes, or if visible from the street a pipe can be covered with wood chase covered with man-made stone or brick as long as proper clearances are maintained.

The diagram at the right shows the ideal location of a heating appliance - located as centrally as possible in the house. This is because convective and radiant heat will be more evenly distributed. The heat moves about whether there are fans running or not, but air circulation is important (see tips below).

Do not expect miracles from your appliance. Rooms farthest away will be cool, but for sleeping this may be ideal. If you have a large home, consider purchasing two appliances to cover heating the square footage of your home.

The diagrams at the right demonstrate how heat is distributed.

Tips:

+ If you have a cathedral ceiling install a ceiling fan and switch the blades to reverse so warm air circulates downward.

+ Add small door fans to circulate heated air through to other rooms.

+ Turn on your furnace fan to circulate heated air throughout the house.

+ For large homes, add a wood stove in the basement. Heat will rise through the floors, stairway, and vents.

+ Install floor grates to allow heat to rise into the rooms above.

Bedroom

Kitchen

Bath

Family Room

Bedroom

Can be used in any home design

Stove or heater

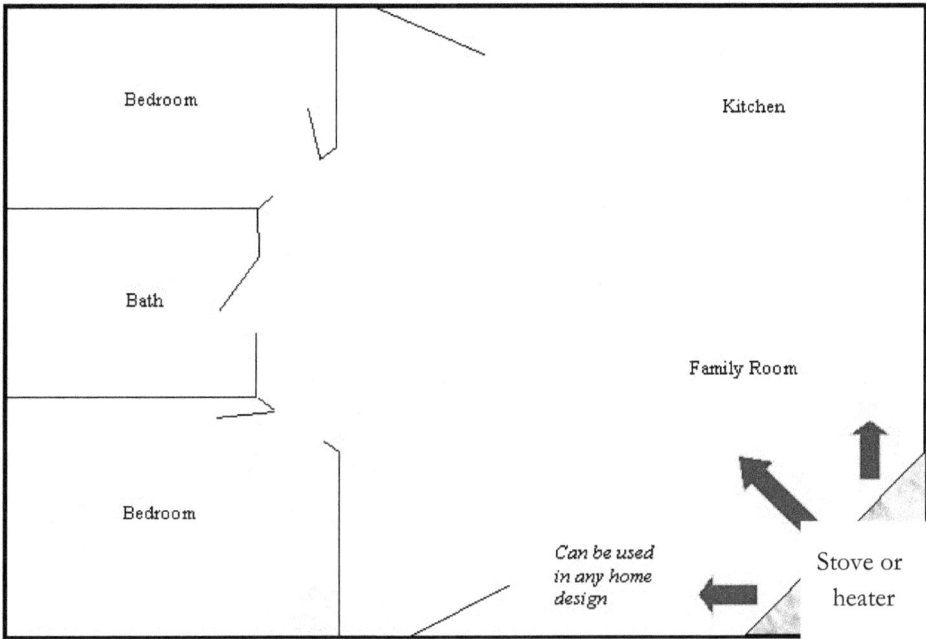

End or corner installation

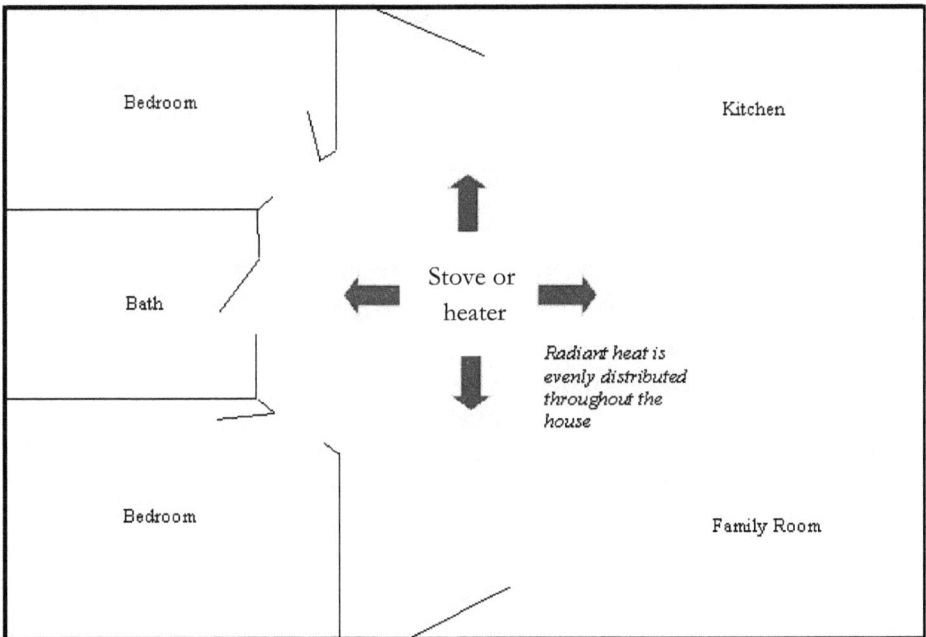

Bedroom

Kitchen

Stove or heater

Bath

Radiant heat is evenly distributed throughout the house

Bedroom

Family Room

Central installation

What Everyone Should Know About Chimney Fires

As chimney technicians, we see a lot of damages by chimney fires. As mentioned previously, most chimney fires are caused by the improper installation of a fireplace insert, however, they can, and do happen with any type of wood-burning appliance.

Most chimney fires occur without the homeowner's knowledge—in fact, only a very few fires are witnessed or reported to the fire department. Fire Department statistics are not complete—since the only reports are those sent in by departments who responded to a fire and are

Photo: Fotolia.com

online. Not all departments, including volunteer fire departments report their statistics.

Some of the damages that can occur are:

- Longitudinal, diagonal, and horizontal breaks in flue tiles.

- Blown out mortar joints or tile sections.

- Holes and mortar bond breaks and cracks in mortar may be found in the smoke chamber area and flue after a chimney fire due to expansion.

- The chimney cover may be warped, discolored, or damaged.

- Stainless steel flue liners, chimney pipe, or Class A chimneys may be buckled, warped, and have separated seams.

- Fires of long duration may cause thermal expansion of the masonry in the cement crown, facial wall, and exterior chimney, which will result in clean breaks in the mortar, bricks, block, or stone.

We often are asked when a fire occurred, which is an impossible thing to do unless the customer remembers the event or the fire department was called out. However, if the cracks in the flue liner are dirty inside, you can safely assume that the fireplace/stove has been used since the fire occurred. Also, don't rule out the possibility that more than one fire has occurred, especially in the case of stove insert installation without positive connection to a steel flue liner.

Sometimes we find broken tile liners in two flues that are right next to each other. In the case where no brick wythe wall is between the liners, and the flues are close together, a chimney fire in one flue can cause a fire in the second flue due to heat transfer, or in some cases, damage the second flue. Clay tiles break when exposed to a quick change in temperature differential of 500 degrees, so only heat is required to break the tiles, not direct contact with fire.

Right: A tile flue liner with longitudinal breaks caused by a chimney fire. The flue was clean since the fire burned off all of the creosote. This does not always occur, and some residual creosote will often be found.

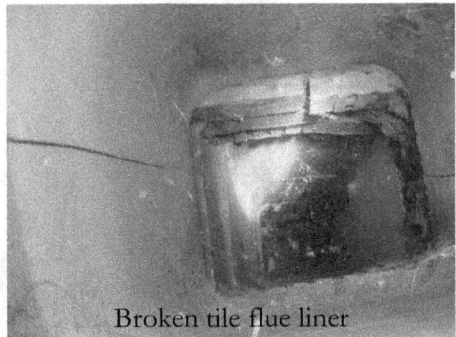

Broken tile flue liner

When a sudden temperature differential of 500 or more degrees occurs in a chimney, the clay tile flue liners usually crack due to expansion. This differential cannot be obtained by the normal operation of a fireplace or wood stove, and has not been able to be duplicated in field study. Industry studies show that a chimney fire is the most likely candidate for the cause of tile liners to break.

Contrary to popular opinion, "hairline" cracks usually go all the way through the tile flue liner. These cracks open up as much a 3/4" of an inch when the flue is heated during use, making an easy path for tar vapors and toxic flue gasses to escape into the space between the flue liner and the exterior chimney chase. If there are any gaps in neighboring flue liners or the chase itself, you can see the potential for hazards.

Carbon Monoxide (CO) is an odorless, tasteless, and invisible by-product of combustion. It occurs when gas or wood is burned. Leakage of CO into the home is a potential for health issues and even death.

After a chimney fire has occurred, contact a professional chimney sweep to evaluate the chimney and appliance for suitability of use, or repairs as needed.

Above: A heavy accumulation of glazed baked-on creosote on the flue walls. A wood-burning stove had been installed without the proper sized flue liner, leaving an extreme fire hazard.

Signs and Symptoms of a Chimney Fire

- The appliance suddenly stops drafting and smoke backs up into the house
- There is a sudden rush of air and loud freight-train like sound
- Flames may shoot out the top or sides of the chimney
- Sounds of flue tiles cracking

What to do after the fire:

- Get everyone out of the house and call 911
- Throw a chimney fire extinguisher on the fire in the firebox
- Close the doors) to the appliance (if applicable)
- After the fire is out, check the attic area for any possible hot areas
- Keep watch for a while- sometimes the fire department does not get all of the embers out and must return
- Call a professional chimney sweep to do an inspection before further use since in most cases there will be severe damage to the interior chimney flue, and in the case of a long-lasting fire, damages to the chimney chase as well that could render the appliance unusable.

As you can see, it is important to avoid having a chimney fire and to do due diligence to make sure this does not happen. The best defense against having a chimney fire is to keep the chimney and connecting pipes well maintained, and serviced by a professional chimney sweep. If you live in an area where no chimney sweep is available, purchase a set of rods and brushes, and do the job yourself. For clay tile flue liners use wire brushes, and for metal chimneys use poly brushes only.

A chimney fire can cause expensive damage to masonry chimneys

Chimney fires are all too common, and often go unnoticed by the homeowner at the time of the event. According to a recent poll by the

Midwest Chimney Safety Council, and average of 1.5 fire-damaged chimneys are found every day that a chimney sweep works if he/she usually sweeps four to five chimneys per day. The number of damaged chimneys that homeowners are unaware of is staggering. In the Kansas City area alone with 2.5 million people, there are a minimum of 25 full-time chimney sweeps working five days per week. Do the math figuring 48 work weeks per year and that calculates to 9,000 chimneys found with damages by chimney fires every year in one metropolitan area alone. That is a lot of chimney fires.

Masonry chimneys are designed to contain a chimney fire in order to keep it from spreading to the rest of the home, that is-- if it is constructed properly with the right clearances. However, once a chimney has been damaged, often with internal damages that are not readily accessible, a second chimney fire is more likely to escape the masonry structure due to gaps created by cracks in mortar and bricks.

Another thing to consider is that masonry, while sturdy and solid, is not impervious to damage by fire, water, creosote, or moisture. Once a chimney is damaged by fire, water will likely leak inside and cause further damage and faster deterioration of the structure. The bricks and mortar may wash out, dampers rust, metal fireplaces rust, internal mortar joints between flue tiles may deteriorate, and often the back wall of a masonry fireplace shows water damage.

In addition to checking the flue, smoke chamber, and damper, the chimney sweep should check the facial wall of the fireplace for fresh breaks that can be caused by expansion due to heat in the smoke chamber area. The smoke chamber is the place where most chimney fires start. Secondarily, the sweep should check all four sides of the chimney in all accessible areas including the attic for fresh breaks caused by expansion. Breaks can be minor or major, but may be related to a chimney fire.

In the photo at the right a chimney fire damaged the internal flue and smoke chamber, as well as the back of the exterior chimney. This area was not visible from the ground and the homeowner had no idea there was so much damage. The chimney was in good condition two years prior as noted in a chimney sweep's evaluation except for the cement crown, which was deteriorating prior to the fire, but had no cracks. A chimney fire occurred, and heat caused the bricks and mortar to expand outward, breaking mortar bonds between bricks and mortar and detaching the cement crown, causing cracks in the crown as well. Since it went unnoticed for a year, rain water further damaged the area as well as the internal part of the structure.

Right: Glazed shiny creosote covering all of the interior flue liner. This usually means that the homeowner is using wet wood or not burning hot enough fires.

Note the Chim-Scan camera inside the flue.

Tips:

♦ Have all woodburning appliance flues swept at least once per year, or twice during the season if used for supplemental or primary heating purposes.

♦ Hire a professional CSIA Certified Chimney Sweep to do the work. He/she will also perform an inspection of the system to be sure it is in working order, which is something the layperson cannot do.

♦ Make sure installations of flue liners are done by a professional who is qualified to do the work. Hire an NFI Certified Wood-burning Specialist or a CSIA Certified Chimney Sweep to do the installation. They will know the critical clearance and installation requirements.

Above: The top portion of this chimney, including the bricks and cement cap expanded and were pushed outward during a chimney fire of long duration. All types of materials expand when they are heated, and if the chimney is cold, this makes it worse. In this case, the top three courses and cement cap had to be rebuilt.

Left: The top portion of this tile liner has burnt creosote and breaks due to a chimney fire.

The inside of a chimney flue with puffed, burnt creosote which expanded during a chimney fire. This is also known as honeycomb creosote. The tiles underneath are almost always broken after a chimney fire.

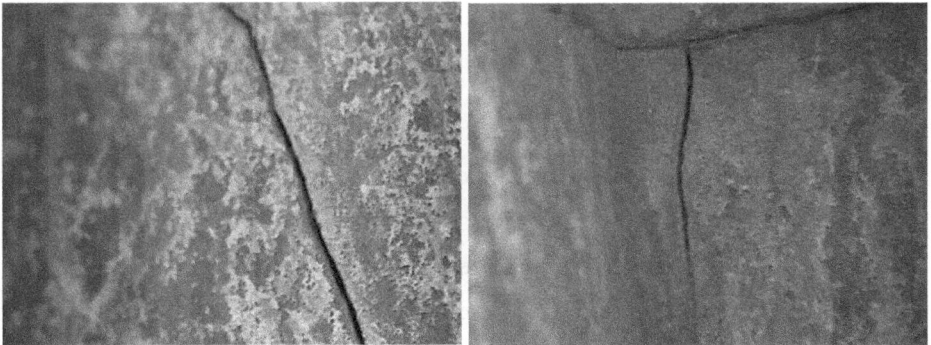

Above: Longitudinal fractures in vitreous clay tile flue liners after a chimney fire.

How to File a Claim for Chimney Fire Damage

Even the best woodturners occasionally have a chimney fire that can cause costly damage to a masonry or metal chimney. Luckily, this type of fire is covered by homeowner's insurance.

♦ Chimney fire damage is a legitimate fire claim and your insurance company is responsible for restoring the chimney to "as was condition." The fire is considered "hostile" or "unfriendly" because it occurred in the chimney flue and chamber, rather than being contained inside the fireplace or stove. Call your insurance agent or adjuster to submit a claim. They will open a case for you and give you a claim number. If you just found out about the fire from a chimney sweep during a routine inspection, tell the adjuster that you had a chimney sweeping or inspection completed and the technician found damages to the chimney that was caused by a chimney fire, and forward the technician's report to your adjuster. Be sure to get the adjusters name, email, and phone number. Note: A chimney sweep cannot file a claim for you—it is the policy holders responsibility to file the claim.

♦ If you know when the chimney fire occurred, i.e. you were home when it happened and you noticed it and/or called the fire department, give the adjuster the date of the fire. If you don't know you won't be able to give them a date but that is OK– most chimney fires go unnoticed at the time they happen and are only found later by an inspector.

♦ Sign the contract for repair and forward the estimate to your adjuster via email. Faxes don't work because the adjuster won't be able to see the photos. Sign the estimate before submitting it for faster claim service.

- Most of the time the insurance company will pay the claim based on the chimney sweep's report (especially if it was a Level 2 inspection with a camera and the proper documentation was submitted), however, for larger claims the adjuster may need to visit the site to see the damages or send an engineer to look at it. Most engineers don't get training on chimneys. You may want to insist that they use the proper Chim-Scan camera equipment to do the evaluation. (Engineers don't get training on chimneys in their standard educational programs)

- Your insurance company may want a second estimate. You can insist that only a qualified licensed contractor do the work because legally the insurance company cannot require that you use any particular contractor, or use an unlicensed or uncertified contractor. Also insist that a permit is pulled and the work is inspected by the building codes official, unless there are no codes in your area.

- If you do have an unlicensed contractor do the repairs and there is a problem, your insurance company is not responsible for having it corrected because you made the choice of contractor to do the work and are responsible for researching their qualifications.

- Most insurance policies have a defined timeline when you must have the repairs completed after you have been made aware of damages—this is usually 6 to 2 months.

- You can ask the adjuster or his/her supervisor to re-open a claim even if it has already been paid. This may be necessary if additional work is needed to complete the repairs once the contractor has opened up the chimney.

- Some insurance companies may try to influence you to use a company based on LOWEST BID. This is illegal. You, as the homeowner, may choose who does the work. And you may insist on having a contractor that is QUALIFIED do the work.

- If you are not getting anywhere with the adjuster, ask to speak to a supervisor. Some adjusters are not familiar with chimney claims and don't understand the repair process. The adjusters use the Exacti-mate system for figuring costs, but that system does not cover all of what is needed to do chimney repair.

♦ Report insurance adjusters or companies who might try to influence you to use a particular company to do the chimney repair, or who will not pay for a claim to restore your fireplace or chimney to its original condition, or who want you to accept repairs that are not up to current NFPA 211 Standards and/or local code requirements to the State Department of Insurance. In our experience, this usually gets results.

♦ If you still have problems, you may want to consult an attorney.

♦ If repairs are not completed this could be a problem when the home is sold in the future and it won't pass inspection when the house is sold.

Water Damage is Chimney Enemy #1

Rain water and condensation are the number one causes of chimney damage, whether it is a masonry chimney or a wood chimney chase serving a manufactured fireplace.

If the chimney is not constructed correctly or maintained properly water can, and will, get inside and wreck havoc on mortar joints, metal dampers, metal fireboxes or smoke domes, older clay tile flue liners, wood framing, metal fireplaces, and masonry.

This chimney was too far gone to save. We had to tear this down and rebuild it with hard bricks.

It is a constant battle to keep water out, but one worth doing to keep a chimney in good working order.

Masonry Chimneys:

Chimney Cover: First and foremost, make sure that the correct size chimney cover is installed on top of every flue liner in the chimney, or have a single custom-made chimney cover made and installed over all flues. In some cases this is the only alternative since some masonry chimney builders install flue liners so close together that it is impossible to fit two or three individual covers side -by-side. Make sure to purchase only a heavy duty stainless steel or aluminum cover that is approved for such use. Inexpensive black steel covers rust and discolor the chimney, and will need to be replaced at some point. A good chimney cover can be purchased from a chimney professional. Generally speaking, the well-made covers are not available in box stores.

Chimney Cap: This is the cement cap (also known as a Crown) at the top of a masonry chimney. It is actually a roof for your chimney made to keep damaging rain water out of the chimney chase interior, and direct water away from the top portion of the masonry. You may notice that the top of your chimney is in bad shape, while the rest looks OK. This is because of the design of the cement cap. Caps without a drip edge allow ran water to flow on to the mortar and bricks or stone right below it, and over time causes the masonry to deteriorate.

Spalling is the term used when brick faces pop off the front of the brick. This us caused when water penetrates the bricks, then freeze/thaw cycles occur causing water to expand and it pushes the brick face off. Unfortunately, once this starts there is already a lot of water inside the bricks. Soft bricks are more susceptible to water penetration than hard bricks. Builders often use soft bricks because they are less expensive, and by the time there is a problem, they are long gone.

If there are only a few spalled bricks, a mason can extract and replace them with new bricks, then apply a professional grade masonry water repellant sealer to the entire exterior of the chimney. Water repellant will help to slow down the deterioration process. Some bricks may continue to spall due to water already inside the bricks. This should be applied every 2-5 years or when water no longer beads up.

Paint traps moisture inside bricks and mortar and only worsens the problem. If you see a painted chimney it is usually because someone is covering up a problem, or a designer decided they didn't like the color of the bricks or stones. We suggest NOT painting a chimney!

Deteriorating and missing mortar joints are a huge issue because once it gets bad enough to where there are cracks or holes in the mortar, or holes water can enter the interior chimney. Not only that, but bats can gain access to a chimney in a hole as small as 1/2" in diameter, as can wasps and bees. We've discovered all kinds of creatures and creepy crawlies inside chimneys that have small holes and cracks.

The best way to avoid costly chimney repair (or rebuilding) is to keep a chimney maintained. Check annually in the spring for any issues and have them taken care of quickly.

Right: A cracked masonry cap is allowing damaging rain water to enter the interior chimney chase.

(Above) This chimney was in poor condition and had to be rebuilt from the roof line up with a new cement cap and drip edge. Note the two new stainless steel chimney covers as well. This is what the top of a masonry chimney should look like.

Why a Cap/Crown with Drip Edge is Best

The International Residential Code requires a drip edge on Caps/Crowns.

Some older chimneys are not built with drip edges, so the top of the chimney will show
deterioration and damage far earlier than the rest of the structure. This is due to rain water running onto the masonry, or in the case of a manufactured chimney, the wood chase.

A crown with a drip edge will give longer life to the chimney. All new crowns must be constructed in this fashion with bond breaks around the flue tiles, mesh for strength, and a slope. Not all masons or chimney contractors know how to build this type of crown so not all offer this type of construction, but it is what you want in order to save money on repair costs. This type of cap is also known as a poured crown, since a form is made first, then cement is poured into the form. It takes longer to build and is more expensive but is worth it in the long run.

Water Repellant is Important

The application of a professional grade water repellant sealer is recommended for all chimneys that have been built with soft type bricks. This will help stop further penetration of water into the masonry. We recommend this for all masonry chimneys no matter their age. Application should be made every 2-5 years or when water no longer beads up on the chimney. Most chimney sweeps do this service.

Chimney Cap/Crown

With no drip edge:
Water sheds directly onto chimney

Chimney Cap/Crown

With drip edge:
Water sheds away from chimney

Note: Since 2012 the International Residential Code requires that all cement caps be built with drip edges. This requires the use of a crown form and curing for three days and a return visit to remove the form. Expect to pay more for this type of cement cap.

Left: This chimney was struck by lightning and needed to be completely rebuilt. This type of damage cannot be repaired.

Left: A gas explosion blew out the back side of this chimney. The client turned on the gas starter, went into the other room to get her husband, then they lit the starter. The couple was okay, the chimney was not.

Close-up of
a spalled
brick

Right: This
chimney was
painted to cover
a problem
before selling
the house. The
new owners
discovered that
the bricks were
spalling and
called us to
inspect it. The
chimney had to
be rebuilt.

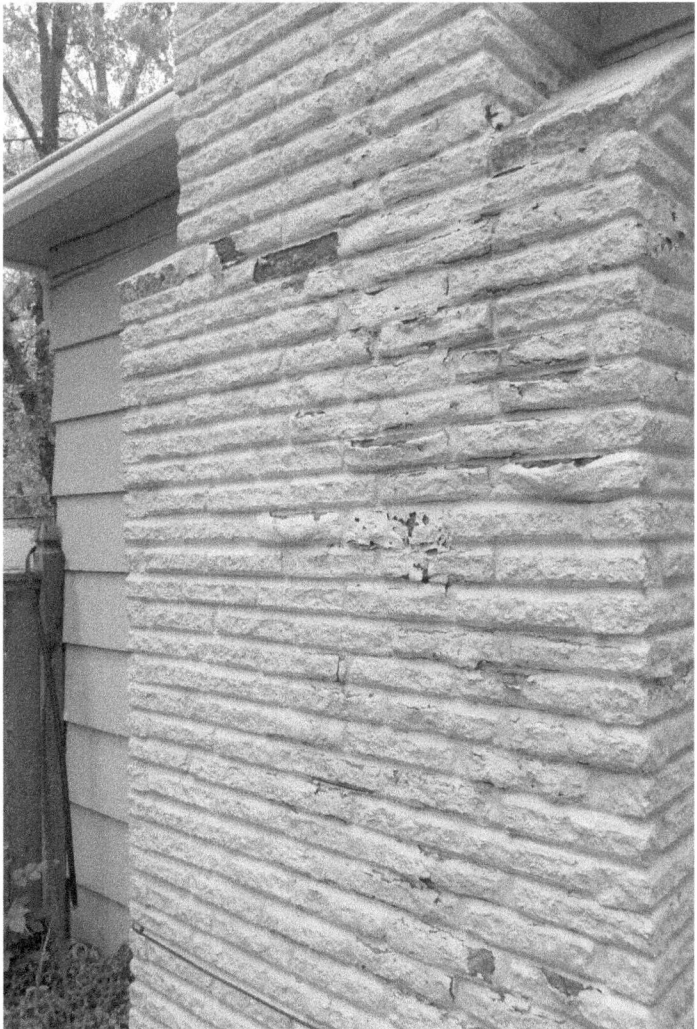

Negative House Pressure Issues

Most homes have negative pressure problems—this is worse in homes that are tightly insulated, or in larger or multi-story houses. Not enough make-up air can get in the house for all of the things that need air, like fireplaces, wood stoves, gas ranges-- and people.

Years ago Gene noticed this problem, but no one in the industry was talking about it. His training in HVAC helped him determine that when a gas furnace or a second fireplace was in use and a fireplace smoked, this meant only one thing - that the house lacked sufficient air for all of the appliances. Gene then developed his own rudimentary solution, then later created a more sophisticated product called the Padgitt WHV. Since then, others have created different types of methods to address house pressure including the Condar Through-the-Wall ventilator which supplies air to an appliance in the room it is in.

When an exhaust fan is used in the kitchen or bath, or the furnace is used, this makes the problem worse.

You may notice cold air drafts coming from fireplaces, fireplaces that smoke, CO backup from the furnace, gas fireplace, water heater, or leaky doors and windows. These are all symptoms of negative pressure in the house. Sometimes unexplained illness can also be a symptom. This is called Sick House Syndrome. The EPA currently estimates that house air is 10 times more unhealthy than outside air.

Negative house pressure is a common problem that can cause fireplaces and wood-burning appliances to smoke, and gas and wood appliances to backdraft deadly Carbon Monoxides. This is probably the least understood house issue, but one that usually can be corrected.

All houses have a positive pressure plane, a neutral pressure plane, and a negative pressure plane. The negative plane is at the lowest portion of the house, and the positive plane is at the upper level, inside the building envelope. The planes move constantly according to pressure changes that occur when someone opens a door or window, or turns a fan or appliance on or off.

House pressure is something that can't be seen with the eye, and the effects are obvious —once a person knows what they are looking for.

A smoking fireplace is a sign of negative house pressure

Signs of negative house pressure include stale air, mold or mildew in bathrooms, unexplained illness among family members or pets, smoking fireplaces or appliances, and condensation on windows. An inadequate amount of fresh air is getting into the house, and this can be a severe health hazard as well as a smoking fireplace problem. The EPA suggests that houses get a full six air exchanges per day for the occupants to breathe.

Tight, or well-insulated houses have a better chance of having a negative pressure problem, and larger homes with multiple stories are likely candidates, however, any house can have a negative pressure problem.

The issue is often first detected by a professional chimney sweep. This is due to the fact that smoking fireplaces are a huge annoyance, and either the sweep will find the problem during a routine inspection, or the homeowner thinks that there is a problem with the fireplace or chimney.

If, after checking for proper chimney construction, including proper height, the flue and smoke chamber sized to code, and stack effect (house taller than the chimney) the next thing to look for is negative house pressure.

There are simple techniques to check for negative pressure as well as complicated methods. First, house pressure should only be tested during cold weather in order to see what is happening when the house is closed up and the heating appliances are used. Next, place shredded lengths of tissue paper or a newspaper over the fireplace opening. Open the damper and watch what happens to the paper. If it moves inward towards the back wall of the fireplace, the draft is established and there is no negative pressure. If the paper moves outward towards the room there is negative pressure. Now open a window in the room very slowly and watch the paper, which should switch to moving inside the fireplace at some point. Measure the window opening and this is the amount of air needed for the fireplace to operate without smoking.

If interested in getting an exact measure of the problem testing can be completed using a Digital Manometer. Some professional sweeps do this testing, otherwise contact an HVAC Professional for this service.

If the house does have a negative pressure issue the next step is to correct or decrease the problem. Other things must be taken in to account are other appliances that use air for combustion and take air from the house like gas furnaces, water heaters, boilers, cooking ranges and ovens, masonry heaters, gas or wood burning stoves, etc. Also, anytime a bathroom or kitchen fan is turned on, this removes air from the home.

Signs of Negative House Pressure

- Sick House Syndrome
- Unexplained headaches
- Unexplained flu –like symptoms that go away when leaving the house
- Pets or young children that are ill for no apparent reason
- Fainting

- Death
- Stale odors
- Mold or mildew in bathrooms
- Condensation on windows
- Smoking fireplaces or stoves that get worse when the gas furnace or a fan kicks on

For more information about CO we suggest visiting www.coheadquarters.com

Solutions to the problem may include the installation of a draft inducing heater which is installed on the flue collar of a stove or insert, and/or installation of a whole-house ventilator.

A whole-house ventilator is not a heat recovery ventilator (HRV) which only provides heated air to the furnace alone.

A *WHV is installed in line with a gas furnace system and operates both actively when the furnace is on, and passively when it is off. The WHV is installed halfway between the furnace and an exterior wall with insulated duct coming from the outside wall to the unit, then pipe is attached to the supply side and return air side of the furnace. Air is heated up in the WHV box before it gets to the heat exchanger so the exchanger will not rust due to condensation.

Why it is Not a Good Idea to Install a Make-up Air Supply Directly to an Appliance

These kits will provide combustion air for the appliance to function, however, it reduces its efficiency by dumping COLD air onto the fire, thereby creating more Carbon Monoxide and negating the purpose of the appliance. Unfortunately, some city codes require this with all new appliances, likely because they are unaware of other methods.

Negative House Pressure

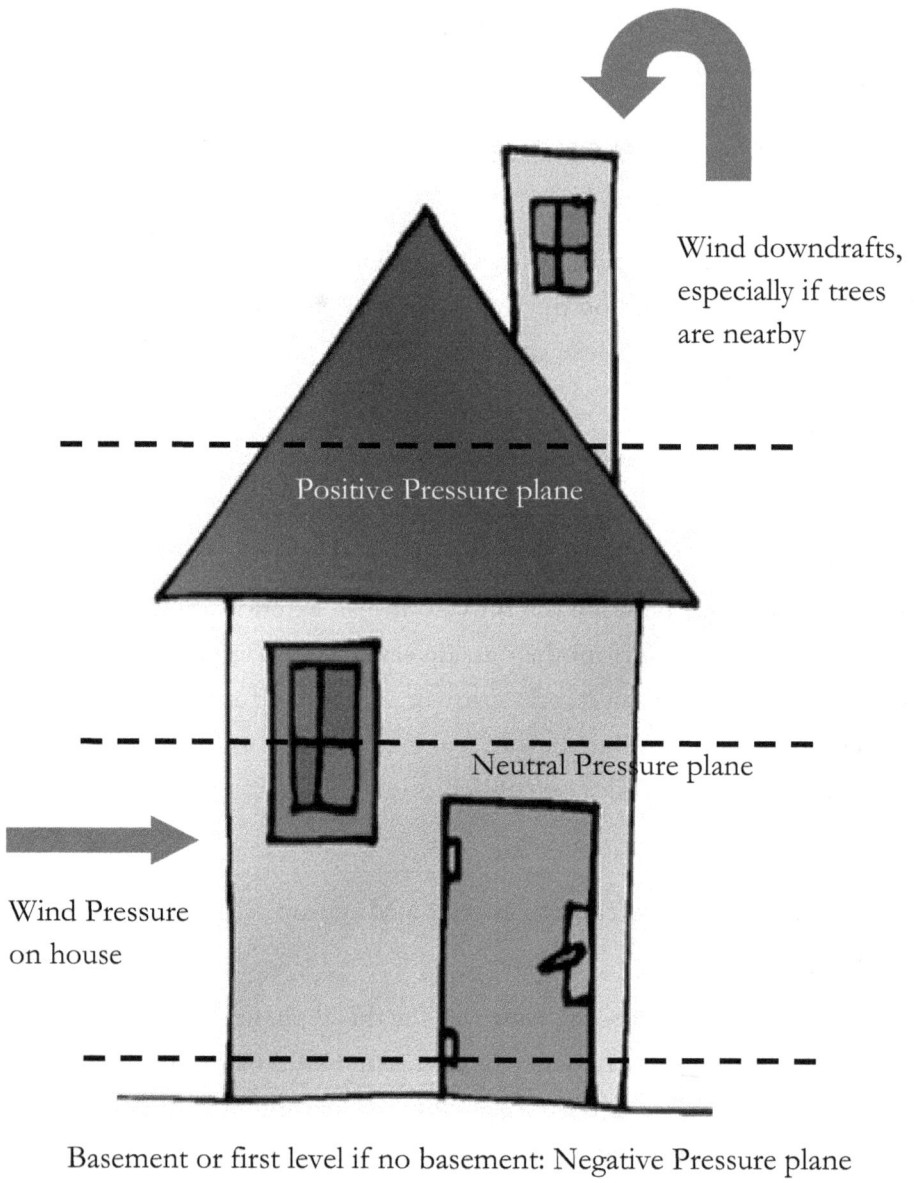

Wind downdrafts, especially if trees are nearby

Positive Pressure plane

Neutral Pressure plane

Wind Pressure on house

Basement or first level if no basement: Negative Pressure plane

Solutions to Negative Pressure Issues

1. The Whole House Ventilator

How it Works:

The WHV system brings in needed air on demand from the house, heats it during the winter months, then distributes it through the house through the cold air returns. This supplies needed combustion air for all appliances in the house including the furnace, hot water heater, and fireplaces. It also re-supplies the house with fresh air when fans are turned on.

An added benefit is fresh air for the occupants to breathe!

Different sizes are available to accommodate any size home.

Installation:

The unit installed between the floor joists in the basement near the furnace, with insulated duct installed to the outside sill plate and the unit. The installer cuts a hole in the sill plate and install a vent cover on the outside. Another duct is installed to the return side of the furnace, and a third duct is installed to the supply side. This is a non-mechanical system and works without electricity. Other systems dump cold air on the heat exchanger, which can cause condensation. The WHV pre-heats the air so no condensation if formed and the heat exchanger is not affected.

This can be installed by an HVAC contractor, chimney professional, or handy homeowner.

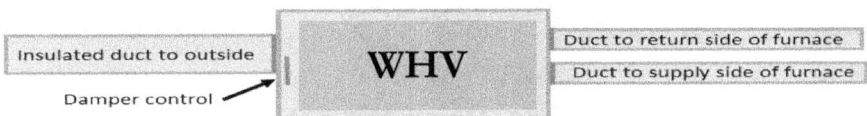

Insulated duct to outside | **WHV** | Duct to return side of furnace / Duct to supply side of furnace

Damper control

The whole-house ventilator concept. Visit www.chimkc.com for more information.

2. Draw Collar

Draw Collar is the brand name for a product that is inserted between the flue take-off and the chimney of a wood-burning stove, or for an insert, between the flue take off and the flue liner. This product can also be used on a masonry heater. It does require electricity to work. The Draw Collar keeps the flue warm so that stoves are easier to start up and do not backup when cooling down. We recommend using one on any stove on the lower level, main level or basement level of the home. The basement is where the negative pressure is worse. It is also advised when a chimney is located on an exterior wall since the chimney will be cold. This product eliminates hard starts and smoking.

Note: A Draw Collar may be needed in addition to a WHV in difficult situations.

How it works: A heater inside the collar automatically comes on when the flue is cold. It uses very little electricity.

A Draw collar on a freestanding woodstove. Photos: Drawcollar.com

3. Outside Air

There are two methods of bringing outside air to an appliance: a Through the Wall outside air kit for the room the appliance is in, or an outside air vent.

Through the wall: Condar manufactures a kit that is installed on an exterior wall in the room the appliance is serving. A damper is used to open or close the vent as needed. This method is preferable to the following.

Outside air vent:

For a fireplace: A mason will create a hole in the masonry and insert a manufactured vent for this purpose.

For a woodstove: Most wood stove manufacturers offer a kit specially made for their appliance.

For an insert: Check with the manufacturer, but we know of none made for these yet.

The drawback: Cold air is dumped onto the fire, which cools it down and makes it less efficient. We recommend avoiding this method unless nothing else works.

Note that in very large houses or severe negative pressure situations more than one method may need to be used to alleviate the problem.

Stack Effect: Something to Think About

Stack effect can occur when the house acts as a better chimney than the chimney does. All of the air within the house is warmer and more buoyant than the air outside and therefore wants to rise. If there is an opening in the uppermost part of the house, the warm air will find it and leak outwards. This creates a powerful draw in the lower part of the home pulling cold air in through the easiest opening; the chimney.

Stack effect occurs in the following situations:

- When a portion of the house is taller than the chimney—even when building codes are followed correctly, the house acts like a chimney, drawing air upward.

- When an room is added to the house and it is taller than the existing chimney. The additional space also changes the pressure dynamics in the house.

- When there are two or more flues in the same chimney and one appliance is being operated—it can pull make up air from the source of least resistance—a fireplace or water heater flue causing smoke a carbon monoxide backup into the home.

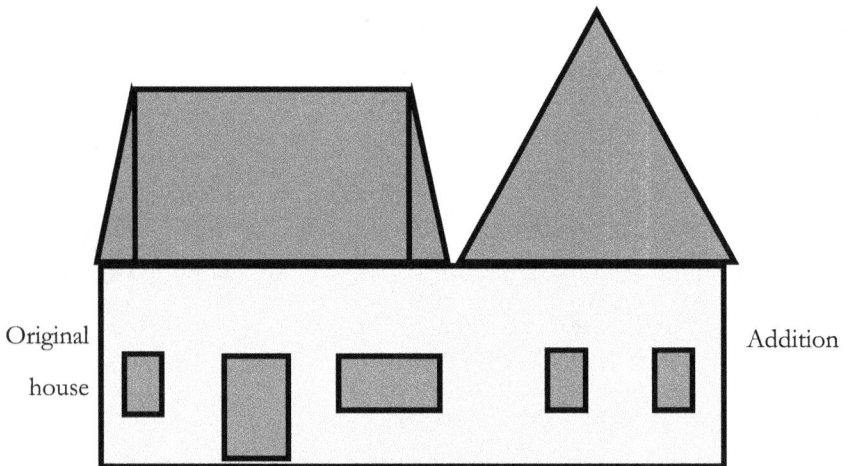

Original house

Addition

In the above diagram the addition is taller than the chimney, so this will cause stack effect. The cure is to raise the chimney higher. Makeup air may also need to be introduced into the house.

Chapter 3
Maintenance Requirements for Wood-Burning Appliances

Operation and Maintenance for Masonry Heaters

Masonry heaters require regular annual maintenance in order to function properly, and avoid chimney fires. Maintenance includes sweeping of the chimney flue, brushing out the flue gas channels to remove fly ash, inspection of the chimney and heater, and doing any repairs necessary.

If the masonry heater is operated properly there should be little, if any creosote in the flue, and you should find only small amounts of soot. If there is any amount of creosote in the flue proper operation and burning procedures should be reviewed. The fire should not be "damped down" to maintain a longer burning time as is the normal procedure with a wood stove. The maximum number of fires per day should be three.

Cleaning the flue gas channels involves using a small poly brush and vacuum. We use dryer vent brush kits. Go to the small channel doors, open them and clean and vacuum each one to remove fly ash. The chimney interior and exterior needs to be inspected, and the heater itself should be inspected for any deterioration or loose firebrick in the firebox, any cracking in the exterior heater skin or finish work, and correct clearances to combustibles. Like any masonry structure, the masonry heater and chimney will need to be maintained and repaired as needed.

A masonry heater is nothing like a wood stove or fireplace and cannot be operated as such.

Get a copy of the **Homeowners Safety Manual and Burning Guide for Masonry Heaters** from the Masonry Heater Association of North America website at www.mha-net.org.

Fires: You may either use a grate or build a fire right on the firebrick hearth based on your preference. The door should be closed during operation, and flammable liquids should not be used to start fires. Homeowners should not burn anything other than dry cord wood in the heater.

Building a top-down burn fire will provide a clean burn start up with less CO and smoke. The top-down burn is the opposite of what you learned as a Scout. Place a couple of large logs on the bottom with air space between them, then add smaller logs on top in the opposite direction, then add kindling. Try Fatwood or dry pine as a fire-starter. The fire will burn down slowly, like a candle. This method warms the flue slowly, and causes draft to establish before the fire really gets going.

A professional chimney sweep is best qualified to sweep and maintain a masonry heater and chimney flue, and can likely do any minor masonry

---

Never Burn Treated Wood!

Manufacturers and professionals suggest using dry cordwood in appliances. As long as it is dried properly, any species of wood will burn well in an appliance. Small pieces of plywood or OSB (oriented strand board, aka "chipboard" or "flakeboard") can also be burned as well.

In contrast, preservative treated wood should never be burned because toxins can be released. For many years, the most common preservative mixture used for treated wood was CCA, a combination of chromium, copper and arsenic. When wood treated with this preservative is burned, some of the arsenic is released into the air with the fly ash, and the rest is concentrated in the ash that remains in the fireplace.

Treated wood is often used for decking, railings and exterior trim. The most common types of treated wood are green in color, and thus usually can be easily identified. These materials should go to the landfill along with ordinary household waste. Treated wood that has been outside for a long time may turn grey and can be hard to identify – if there is any doubt as to whether it is treated wood, throw it out. Wood that has been painted also should not be burned.

Some wood species such as cedar, redwood, cypress and black locust are used outside because they naturally contain chemicals which protect them from insect and fungal attack. It is perfectly safe to burn these woods. If using pallet wood—be sure it is untreated wood.

Using wood "waste" as a fuel for fires is common in the wood products industry and is perfectly acceptable at home too. Just be sure to put painted and preservative treated wood in the garbage, rather than into the fireplace.

Do not Transport Firewood from Other Areas

Transporting firewood outside the area where you burn could spread devastating non-native invasive species according to the Nature Conservancy and the National Forest Service.

When firewood is moved pests that go along with it may include the European gypsy moth, the Asian long-horned beetle, the Emerald Ash Borer, and pathogens such as beech bark disease, sudden oak death pathogen, and several others.

Campers and travelers are urged to purchase or cut their firewood locally and to leave any excess wood at the site to avoid the spread of these infestations.

Some states and counties don't allow you to transport firewood across their borders.

The Emerald Ash Borer is a very small insect that originated in China and was transported in solid wood packing material used in cargo shipment. The larvae feed under the bark of Ash trees, leaving S shaped marks. They can wipe out an entire neighborhood with in a few years.

All wood-burning freestanding stoves, fireplace inserts, circulating fireplaces, and Rumford style fireplaces require annual sweeping to remove flammable creosote.

ALL WOOD CREATES CREOSOTE—even dry hardwoods. There is no way around it.

All creosote is flammable, but third stage or glazed baked on creosote is the most flammable and needs to be avoided at all costs.

There are three stages of creosote: Stage 1 is very fine and can be removed easily. Stage 2 is chunky and takes extra elbow grease to remove. Stage 3 is impossible to remove with regular brushing methods and must be removed with a rotary chain system, or a chemical creosote remover which may require several trips. In some cases with baked on glazed creosote, it just easier and less expensive to extract the tile flue liner and start over with a stainless steel liner. If a new small flue liner is inserted into an existing tile flue liner be sure any creosote is removed first due to the potential for fire.

WE DO NOT RECOMMEND CHIMNEY SWEEPING LOGS

As chimney professionals, we have seen what happens when this log is used. Creosote flakes off and falls down to the smoke shelf, where it sits closer to the fire. Then, a chimney fire can occur when a spark reaches it. A couple of our customers had chimney fires the day after using this log. And the log cannot perform an inspection of the chimney!

Wax Firelogs: We do not recommend using a wax firelog in any appliance as it creates a waxy substance that creosote clings to more easily and it is difficult to remove from flue walls. Never use this type of log as a starter in a wood-burning stove or insert.

Keep creosote to a minimum by performing regular chimney sweeping. Be sure to remove creosote from the flue walls, smoke chamber, and connecting pipes. A professional should do this job.

Keep creosote down by spraying ACS (Anti-Creo-Soot) or similar product on the logs before each burn.

Remove ashes from the ash pan below a wood stove by taking them outside in a covered ash bucket, then leave on a non-combustible surface for several days before disposing of the ashes. Embers can stay hot for days, and cause a fire if placed in a trash container too early. You may wish to spread the ashes out in your garden to enhance the soil.

Remove ashes from a stove insert from the interior of the firebox. There usually is no ash pan with inserts.

Clean the glass door using Speedy White or other cleaner, or place a damp paper towel in ashes and scrub the glass with that. The glass will come clean. Only clean glass when it is cool!

Sweeping a chimney yourself

If you live in an area where there are no professional chimney sweeps you'll have no choice but to do this job yourself. If you have a clay tile flue liner purchase a wire brush sized to the liner. The most common sizes are 13" x 13" and 9" x 13". If you have a stainless steel chimney purchase a poly brush. Wire brushes can cause damage to stainless steel chimney pipe. Purchase a set of rods so that you have enough to reach the top of the flue. Close the damper and sweep the chimney from the outside through the access door, if there is one. Otherwise tarp off the front of the fireplace and run a shop vac in the fireplace to capture dust. Brush the flue slowly, going up and down until all of the creosote is removed from the flue.

After the creosote is removed use a drop light and a mirror to inspect the interior. Ideally, a chimney camera would be used for this purpose, but these are very expensive. If you see any cracks in the flue tiles or missing mortar joints between the liner sections discontinue using the fireplace until it can be inspected by a professional. (See the section on chimney fire damage)

Removing soot stains from bricks and stone

Soot stains over a fireplace can ruin a focal point in a room and detract from the beauty of the stone, tile, or brick facing. Long thought to be irremovable, there are some new techniques and products that can do the job.

Soot stains are one of the most difficult stains to remove, especially if bricks or stones are porous rather than hard. But it is worth a try no matter what type of masonry is used to frame a fireplace opening. The first thing to consider is that plain water should never be used on soot because it will make the problem worse.

First, vacuum the stained area using a small nozzle or brush to remove as much of the soot as possible. Then try one of the following products:

Soot Eraser: This is an item manufactured by Hy-C Company in St. Louis, Missouri, and is available at hearth retailers, hardware stores, and from chimney sweeps. The product looks like a big eraser or sponge, and when used to wipe stone or brick it often

takes the soot off. The soot eraser works on most surfaces including woodwork, walls, blinds, and shades in addition to masonry.

Speedy White Hearth & Stove Cleaner: This product can be used to remove soot from glass doors, tiles, metal, and masonry. Speedy White also works on cloth, vinyl, carpeting, plastics, grills, and fiberglass. It comes in spray container and is available from hearth retailers or chimney sweeps. The product is sprayed on then wiped off with a soft cloth.

DIY Degreaser: Mix up a degreasing solution by placing 1 tablespoon of Tri-sodium phosphate in a 1 gallon bucket of warm water. Protect the floor with plastic and put on safety glasses and heavy duty rubber gloves. Open windows and run a fan facing out the window. Wipe the stain off in one direction using a sponge. Rinse out the sponge after each pass. Do not scrub or the soot stain may become worse.

Paint-N-Peel: This is a newer environmentally friendly product and service which is available from professional chimney sweeps, who will first protect glass doors, then apply the product to the masonry. The product works on marble, granite, slate, tile, concrete, mortar, brick, and stone. It works best on smooth hard surfaces. The sweep will return 24 hours later to slowly peel the dried product from the masonry, taking soot with it. The product is like a very thick paint with absorption qualities. Use for difficult to remove soot stains. Depending on the type of masonry more than one application may be necessary. Paint –N-Peel is available from retailers, but it takes some training to do the job right so a professional should do the application and removal.

Next, try to figure out why the soot stains occurred in the first place. The most common reason is that a damper was not opened prior to using a fireplace. This happens more often than most people think! The second most common reason is not so apparent and has to do with house pressures. During cold months when the house is closed up negative pressure is at its worse. The condition can cause fireplaces to smoke and soot up fireplace faces. This is something that should be tested by a professional chimney sweep during cold weather in order to get accurate readings. If the house is found to be under negative pressure the sweep may be able to offer a solution by installing a whole house ventilator. See the section about Negative House Pressure for more information.

HEATING SAFETY TIPS

Avoid fire and burns during the heating season by following these tips.

- Don't burn pine trees, railroad ties, or wet wood since they create excessive amounts of flammable creosote.

- Have the chimney checked annually (every 1-2 months during the heating season if used for the primary source of heat) and cleaned as necessary by a professional CSIA Certified Chimney Sweep to remove flammable creosote and inspect the system. (www.csia.org)

- Most fires in wood stove and fireplace flues occur because of a lack of regular cleaning to remove creosote, which is the residue left behind by unburned fuel (ALL fuel burns incompletely– even hardwoods).

- Burn only seasoned, dry wood for more complete combustion and less creosote accumulation. Hard or soft wood is ok, soft pine is not good to burn.

- Follow operating instructions by the manufacturer (if applicable) to assure safe and efficient heating.

- Never use flammable liquids to start a fire—the fumes can ignite and explode. Use an approved gel, fatwood, or Firestarter instead.

- Remove flammable materials such as stockings from the mantel before starting a fire.

- Ashes can still smolder after several days. Use a metal container to transport ashes to the exterior of the home and leave on a noncombustible surface to cool before disposal.

- Do not overfire or build large fires in open fireplaces in an attempt to heat your house. Fireplaces are listed as "decorative appliances" and are meant for small, ambient fires for a short time only. Over-firing can cause nearby hidden combustible framing to ignite.

- Open fireplaces are not energy efficient. If you want to make your fireplace energy efficient, have a wood or gas fireplace insert installed by a professional. Do NOT install a fireplace insert without a stainless steel flue liner.

- If a chimney fire occurs, throw a chimney fire extinguisher in the fire, close the damper (if possible), get out of the house, and call the fire department. DO NOT use the chimney until it has been inspected by a Certified Chimney Sweep for fire-worthiness.

- Chimney fires can cause damages to the flue, smoke chamber, crown, and sometimes brickwork. Damage from a fire can make the system more unsafe and allow a subsequent fire to escape into the attic or framing.

- Do not leave open fires unattended.

- Keep a chimney fire extinguisher next to any wood-burning appliance.

- Don't burn treated wood, railroad ties, trash, or colored paper since they emit toxic fumes.

- Have a heavy duty stainless steel chimney cover installed to keep damaging rain, animals, and flammable nests and debris out of the chimney.

- Keep combustible materials (including furniture) at least 3' away from the appliance.

- A screen should be placed in front of open fireplaces to keep embers and sparks from popping out.

- Place a child guard screen around stoves to keep young children from getting burned.

Cures for Hard-Starting Wood Stoves

In the middle of winter when temperatures are very cold and the wind is biting, a nice cozy fire to warm up to is what many people look forward to at the end of the day. But some wood-burning stoves just won't start, or take forever to get going, and that can be extremely frustrating.

We had this issue once when my husband started up the wood stove at 630 p.m. after we had both been out all day. The stove was cold, there were few embers left from the morning fire, and the temperature outside was 22 degrees not counting the wind chill factor. The Class A stainless steel chimney was very, cold and the stove just didn't want to start.

There are several factors that can affect wood stove starts:

Cold air falls, so the air in the chimney pushes downward, making it more difficult to get a stove started on very cold days. This applies to metal chimneys and masonry chimneys.

Inadequate air supply will hinder or make it impossible to get a fire going.

Wet wood is hard to start and burn and should never be used.

Stoves located on lower levels are affected by negative house pressure.

Solutions to these issues can involve opening a door or window to get adequate air needed to start the stove, or installation of a whole-house ventilator to be sure that there is adequate air for the house in general, and for the stove in particular. If the stove is located on a lower level negative pressure will also work against it, so the installation of a chimney pipe heater will likely be necessary. The heater can be installed on a stove on any level to make starting easier. What the heater does is keep the chimney warm so that draft is easy to establish, and it also kicks in when the stove is cooling down so that there is no smoke backup.

Always use dry wood (hard or soft) with 20% or less moisture content. Investment in an inexpensive moisture meter will assure that the wood is dry enough to burn.

Start a fire using very small pieces of kindling or Fatwood (dry pine). Start a fire using the top-down burn method with

Moisture meters cost about $20

kindling on top and larger pieces below it. This method makes the fire burn longer and is more efficient and easier to start.

When planning location of a wood stove, try to place the stove in the center part of the house and have less chimney exposed to the exterior. Besides being the best location to distribute heat evenly throughout the home, the less outside exposure for the chimney the better. The house will keep the pipe warmer and make it easier to start a wood-burning stove and keep the fire going.

Starting up your Wood Stove:

When starting a wood stove, install wood first using the top-down burn method to set it up. Open up the air supply doors fully to let in as much air as possible. Crack open a door or window. It takes about 10-15 minutes to get the fire going well. After the fire is going, slowly close the air supply, leaving enough of an opening for the fire to keep going without having roaring flames. A fire that is too hot can cause overheating of the stove and/or a chimney fire. Keep a stove thermometer on the stove to regulate temperature, which should be between 400 – 600 degrees.

Invest in an inexpensive Stove Thermometer to keep tabs on the temperature. The Stove Thermometer magnetically connects to the stove top, door or flue pipe to show at a glance if the stove is operating within an efficient burning range.

Tips for Refurbishing an Old Cast Iron Stove

If you're brave enough to tackle this project yourself instead of sending a family heirloom stove out to a professional, here are some tips:

Make sure the stove is in good condition before starting the project. The interior is the most important. If the firebox needs to be repaired get that done first. Brush the entire surface of the stove with a course rotary drill brush to remove rust. Next, using a 0-gauge steel wood pad rub the surface of any remaining rust spots using a circular motion. Apply stove polish with a toothbrush in a circular motion until the entire stove is coated. Allow to dry for 24 hours, then apply a second coat and allow it to dry for another 24 hours. Using a fine wire brush in a rotary drill buff the surface of the stove, then rub the stove with a fine cloth.

Choosing, Prepping, and Storing Firewood

Choosing the right type of wood and drying it properly is important to the operation and performance of a wood-burning appliance. Green firewood may contain 50% or more water by weight. It produces less heat because heat must be used to boil off water before combustion can occur. Green or wet wood also produces much more smoke and creosote than dry wood. For these reasons—never burn wet wood.

Firewood should always be purchased dry or allowed to dry before burning. The best way to assure this is to purchase or cut it down it at least six months in advance and leave it in the woods, then stack it allowing for air circulation for another six months to dry. Leaving the cut wood in the woods for six to twelve months allows the oils to dissipate and any bugs or critters to leave the wood and not travel home with you.

Stack wood in an area that gets a lot of sunlight rather than shade. Orient wood so that the cut ends face the direction of the prevailing wind.

In the Unites States wind usually moves from west to east but if you live in a valley, wind direction may vary based on warm air rising,. Take a cue from deer and face wood in the direction they move.

Be mindful of what your woodpile looks like. The neighbors may complain to the city if it is unkempt or offer praise if it is straight and neat. If you really want to impress passersby, stack the wood in a cool design (there are some amazing creations on the internet).

The woodpile should be kept off of the ground to avoid rot. This can be accomplished by using bricks, blocks, or treated 4 x 4's placed lengthwise on the ground.

Arrange wood with gaps between the pieces so that air can circulate. Stack split pieces bark side up to shed moisture. To support the pile use a purchased holder or standing trees, fence posts, or rebar driven into the ground. Stack in one log thick racks for faster drying. The old myth about keeping the wood pile some distance away from any buildings to avoid termites and carpenter ants is not true. The queen lives underground and without her the critters are harmless. However, brown recluse spiders do love woodpiles so that is reason enough for me to keep the wood pile at least 25' from the house. Always use gloves to handle wood to avoid an unwelcome bite.

Be sure to make a roof of some type, whether from a tarp or even a roof built of shingles to keep water and snow off of the wood, keeping in mind that the sides need to be open to allow for air movement. More industrious wood burners may want to build a more sturdy and permanent structure with posts and a roof.

When bringing wood indoors for use, leave it near the stove or fireplace for a couple of days to further remove moisture (keep wood at least 36" away from the opening).

The difference between soft woods such as fir, cedar, alder and other hard wood such as white oak, mulberry, or walnut is density. The heavier hard woods contain more heat per volume, therefore less wood is needed and loading (putting wood on the fire) is less frequent. This is especially important for wood-burning stove users because the burn time is longer and more efficient.

Some firewood dealers sell "mixed hardwood" or mixed soft and hardwood" firewood. This may or may not be desirable, depending on the proportion of low- density hardwoods that are included., so be sure to ask what types of woods and at what proportion will be in the mix. Softwoods are less desirable, so the price will be less than for hardwoods.

When purchasing firewood be sure to ask if you are getting a full cord, face cord, rick, or pickup load as the volume varies greatly. A full cord measures eight feet wide by four feet deep and four feet high and is 128 cubic feet in volume.

Firewood has been bought and sold this way since colonial times. A face cord, sometimes called a rick, measures eight feet wide by four feet high by depth depending on cut length. Cut length is usually 12—18" long. You may request cut length at the time of purchase to fit your stove.

A pickup load is generally 64 cubic feet in volume depending on if it is stacked or piled in. A randomly piled load will have less wood content. Ask the wood dealer if he will split the wood for you and if not, you will need to split the larger pieces so they will dry properly.

Basically, all wood has the same BTU's per pound, but serious wood-burners who use an appliance such as a wood-burning stove or masonry heater burn hardwoods which offer a longer burn time and less time splitting. *Hedge and Hemlock are not recommended* due to the amount of sparks emitted. Hedge burns very hot and can damage wood-burning stoves. If you must use hedge, mix with other wood types.

To insure wood is dried to 20% or less moisture content, use an inexpensive moisture meter to test it. If no meter is available, bang two pieces of cut wood together. If they sound hollow and loud, the wood is dry. If the sound is a low thud the wood is still wet.

You'll need an axe, a set of splitting wedges, and a maul in order to split your own firewood. To make the task easier, purchase a manual or hydraulic log splitter ($40—$200), or a gas-powered long splitter ($1,000 +).

Make kindling by splitting some cordwood into very small pieces. Dry pine is great for kindling purposes.

Fatwood is a very good fire starter with only 2-3 pieces needed to start a fire using one match. Fatwood is derived from the heartwood or center of pine trees and is loaded with pine resin which is very flammable. Harvest fatwood from the center of pine stumps or purchase from hearth dealers or chimney sweeps.

How to Stack and Store Firewood

Experienced wood-burners have a few tried and tested methods for storing firewood that can prevent wood from rotting and dry it out efficiently. Choosing the right wood, and cutting, and splitting properly are also factors to take into consideration to prepare for the next season.

When cutting wood in the forest look for dead trees first before cutting down a good healthy tree. Make sure the tree has not rotted out, then cut

Left:

This is a good way to store firewood. Keep it sheltered but let air circulate

into lengths appropriate for the fireplace or wood stove. Next, split larg-er logs in to pieces so that the interior wood is exposed to the air. Wood that has not been split will not dry out. Spitting wood is good exercise, but there are hand mechanical, electric, and gas-powered wood splitters available from $150 to $1,000 to make the job easier.

The next step is to prepare a location for the stacked wood that is away from the house and open on both sides to allow for wind to blow through and dry the wood out. Place 2 x 4s or blocks on the ground lengthwise, then stack the wood loosely in rows. By not placing wood directly on the ground it won't rot out.

Place rebar or other support in the ground at each end of your firewood stack to hold the wood in place. Cover with a tarp or lean-to to keep weather off of the top of the wood while allowing air to circulate through the ends.

Let wood dry for at least 6 -12 months before burning!

Wet wood at more than 20% moisture content uses a lot of energy to dry the wood out before it will burn. For this reason, an inexpensive moisture meter is a good investment.

Bring pieces of wood indoors several days before burning and place a couple of feet away from the side of the wood stove to dry it out even further.

The Top-Down Burn

This may be the opposite of what you are used to doing, but the top-down burn burns more efficiently with less pollutants.

To start a fire, place 2-3 large logs on the bottom, then 2-3 medium sized logs, then very small pieces of wood, and finally kindling. Add a couple of pieces of Fatwood to the top and light the fatwood with a match. This is the top-down burn method which has been proven to be cleaner burning and longer lasting. Fatwood is the center part of the pine tree and lights very easily. This method also makes for a more efficient and clean-burning fire with less Carbon Monoxide emissions.

Best Quality Woods Chart

(Information obtained from the University of Missouri Extension Center and Utah State

Wood Species	Dry Weight (lbs./ Cord)	Heat per Cord (Million BTUs)	Ease of Split- ting	Smoke	Sparks	Coals	Overall Quality
Apple	3888	**27.0**	Medi-	Low	Few	Good	Excellent
Ash, Green	2880	20.0	Easy	Low	Few	Good	Excellent
Alder	2540	17.5	Easy		Mod-	Good	
Ash, White	3472	**24.2**	Medi-	Low	Few	Good	Excellent
Aspen, Quaking	2160	18.2	Easy		Few	Good	
Basswood (Linden)	1984	13.8	Easy	Medium	Few	Poor	Fair
Beech	3760	**27.5**	Diffi-		Few	Excellent	
Cherry	2928	20.4	Easy	Low	Few	Excellent	Good
Chestnut		18.0	Medi-				Good
Coffee Tree, Kentucky	3112	21.6	Medium	Low	Few	Good	Good
Dogwood	4230	High	Diffi-		Few	Fair	
Douglas-fir	2970	20.7	Easy	High	Few	Fair	Good
Hackberry	3048	21.2	Easy	Low	Few	Good	Good
Honey Lo-	3832	**26.7**	Easy	Low	Few	Excellent	Excellent

Wood Species	Dry Weight (lbs./ Cord)	Heat per Cord (Million BTUs)	Ease of Splitting	Smoke	Sparks	Coals	Overall Quality
Locust, Black	4016	**27.9**	Difficult	Low	Few	Excellent	Excellent
Maple, Other	3680	**25.5**	Easy	Low	Few	Excellent	Excellent
Mulberry	3712	**25.8**	Easy	Medium	Many	Excellent	Excellent
Oak, Bur	3768	**26.2**	Easy	Low	Few	Excellent	Excellent
Oak, Red	3528	**24.6**	Medium	Low	Few	Excellent	Excellent
Oak, White	4200	**29.1**	Medium	Low	Few	Excellent	Excellent
Osage-orange	4728	**32.9**	Easy	Low	Many	Excellent	Excellent
Sycamore	2808	19.5	Difficult	Medium	Few	Good	Good
Walnut,	3192	22.2	Easy	Low	Few	Good	Excellent

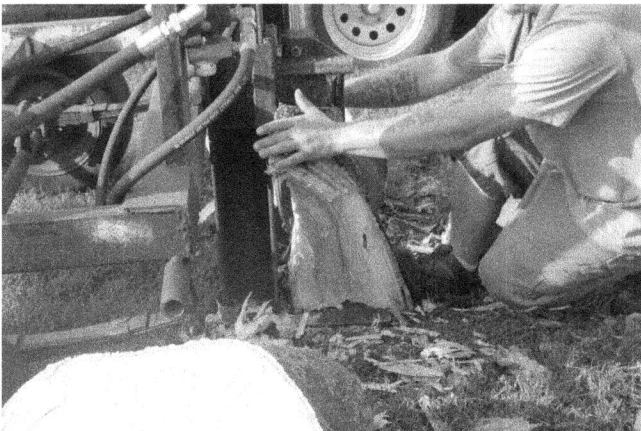

TIP:

Splitting firewood is much easier with a firewood splitter. This one is gas-powered but there are many options available.

U.S. Home Heating Residential Fuel Prices
2014-2015 (From Inspectipedia)

Fuel Type	Recent Price	Units	Source & comments
Natural gas prices	$10.21 [1]	K CuFt [2]	U.S. E.I.A. 49% of homes use natural gas
No. 2 home heating oil	$2.80	US Gallon	U.S. E.I.A. 6% of homes use NO. 2 oil
LPG/Propane Price	$1.83	US Gallon	U.S. E.I.A. 6% of homes use propane
Electricity prices	$0.1246 (12.46 cents)	KWH [3]	U.S. E.I.A. 4% of homes heat with electricity
Firewood price	$230	Full Cord	Web survey of vendors Feb 5 2015. 2% of U.S. homes heat primarily by wood
Other			1% of homes use other heating methods
Pellet Fuel	$5.22	40 Lb Bag	Walmart Price quoted 5 Feb 2015. U.S. Tractor Supply quotes $5.29
Coal	$53. -> $11.55	Ton	U.S. E.I.A., Coal prices range by area and coal type, including coal SO² levels. BTUs per ton also varied from 12.5K BTU/pound to 8.8K BTU/pound where prices roughly also track BTU

Material Comparison Chart

Material	Thermal Conductivity W/MK (Btu-in/hr-ft²-°F)	Specific Heat Kj/Kg/°C (Btu/lb-°F	Density
Soapstone	6-7 (42-48)	-.94 (0.23)	3.05
Granite	-3 (20.08)	.09 (1.192)	2.9
Cast Iron	75 (520)	0.660 (0.16)	6 - 8

When wood is "checked" (cracked) it is an indication that it is dried out
sufficiently to use in an appliance.

Fatwood Firestarter gets fires going easily.
Alternatively, chop dry pine in to small pieces.

Chapter 4
What You Need to Know About Chimneys

A chimney is needed for any type of wood-burning appliance. The chimney and its flue has two functions: To remove toxic flue gasses and smoke from the home and away from people and to provide draft so the fire keeps going. The chimney is critical to the function of the appliance.

Masonry chimneys need regular maintenance, like everything else in the home. A professional chimney sweep should inspect the chimney and flues annually and sweep as necessary to remove flammable creosote. All gas and wood-burning flues serving furnaces, water heaters, and fireplaces have annual wear and tear. The inspector will check for clogs, gaps, cracks, and correct sizing to be sure there is no Carbon Monoxide leakage or backup.

If the mason did not use the correct mortar between the tile flue liner sections, it will eventually wash out and need to be replaced. This can be expensive, and is unfortunately very common.

If soft bricks are used rather than hard bricks, the chimney will deteriorate over a short period of time, spall, and eventually need to be rebuilt. Spalling is the term used for brick faces popping off due to excessive moisture penetration of the bricks. This cannot be repaired and the bricks must be replaced. If there are more than a few spalled bricks on a chimney it will likely need to be partially or completely rebuilt. Most damage is found near the top of the chimney where it is exposed to weather. Damage to masonry can also occur faster if a cement cap with a drip edge is not used, as was the case in the photo above. This wasn't required until 2012 in the International Residential Code.

Masonry chimneys and fireplaces are very long-lasting and beautiful, and with the right choice of brick or stone and design of the structure, complement the home's exterior and interior. The home builder should take a cue from the neighborhood and won't go wrong with the choice of a masonry chimney if other nearby chimneys are also masonry.

The brick chimney above is venting a fireplace and a furnace/water heater. The staining on the bricks was caused by an old rusty chimney cover. Rust stains are nearly impossible to remove.

Tip:

To keep masonry chimneys in good shape, have a professional grade masonry water repellant sealer applied every 2-5 years.

We mentioned this earlier but thought it was worth saying again. Here is an other example of a brick chimney that was spalling badly (brick faces popping off because the chimney was built with soft bricks, and later painted.. Paint traps moisture inside the bricks and only makes the problem worse. n this case, the chimney is in such bad condition that it couldn't be saved and must be torn down and rebuilt.

Right: A stainless steel flue liner installed into a clay tile flue liner serving a wood-burning appliance.

Chimney Height is Critical to Appliance Performance

Fireplaces and wood-burning stoves only work right when everything is built or installed correctly, and that includes the height of the chimney. There are several factors to take into consideration when planning for the termination height of a masonry or factory built chimney system.

When building, or rebuilding, a chimney the builder should check the height to be sure that it not only conforms to National Fire Protection 211 Standards, which is the standard used in the industry for chimney construction, but also conforms to International Residential Code requirements. Both the standard and the code require that a chimney be three feet taller than the high side of the roof where it exits, and two feet taller than anything (roof, trees, dormers, etc.) within ten feet. This is the first step in determining what the finished height of the chimney should be. If a fireplace smokes, the height of the chimney could be a factor.

Short flues: Additionally, keep in mind that a short flue (under 12') may not draft correctly, so the chimney height may need to be extended if a fireplace is on an upper level of the home. It is generally accepted in the industry, although not a code requirement that flues under 12 or 15 feet in height may not draft well. This may mean that the chimney height needs to be taller than code requires so it will function properly.

Stack effect: The second factor to consider is the construction of the home. If a chimney is located on a room addition or end of a house, and the main section of the house is taller than the chimney, the house will act like a chimney and pull air upwards. This can cause what is known as "Stack Effect," and pull smoke back in to the house from the fireplace while it is in operation, and smells when it is not in use. For this reason, always plan the location of a chimney carefully.

Trees: If trees or branches are within ten feet of the chimney they can affect draft and cause downdrafts. If necessary, have trees and limbs cut back further than ten feet away.

What not to do: Don't ever add a section of tile flue liner to the chimney to make it taller without extending the exterior brick chase at the same time. Flue liner joints must be below the exterior chase in order to prevent them from falling over, and if installed incorrectly can be a hazard.

Homeowners may want to consult with their professional chimney sweep before adding a room addition or constructing a new home to determine the best location for the chimney and fireplace. In some cases, the chimney simply cannot draft correctly due to the location and house construction, and it may need to be built higher, or removed altogether. An alternative fireplace, such as a direct vent gas insert, may be a good alternative to an open wood-burning fireplace in some cases. Direct vent fireplaces are closed sealed systems that use outside air for combustion and are not as affected by the house construction as open fireplaces.

How to plan a chimney for your wood-burning appliance per IRC Code and NFPA 211 Standards

First, measure to see how much chimney pipe will be needed. Keep in mind the 3-2-10 rule that must be followed or the chimney will not draft properly:

3-2-10 RULE:

The chimney must terminate at least 3' higher than the highest point of the roof where it exits AND be 2' taller than any part of the roof or other structure within 10' of the chimney. This may still not be adequate if a portion of the house is taller than the chimney (as with room additions) and you may need to make the chimney taller. The IDEAL location for a chimney is inside the building envelope, not on an outside wall. If you can only install on an outside wall, you may want to consider building a frame around the chimney with insulation inside, wire mesh to keep the insulation away from the pipe. Remember to adhere to proper clearances or a house fire could result.

Masonry Chimney Construction

If using a masonry chimney, whether unlined or tile lined, a single-wall UL listed insulated chimney liner must be used with a wood-burning heating appliance. In most cases, the liner can be installed inside the existing tile liner, however, if there is not enough clearance the tile liner might need to be removed.

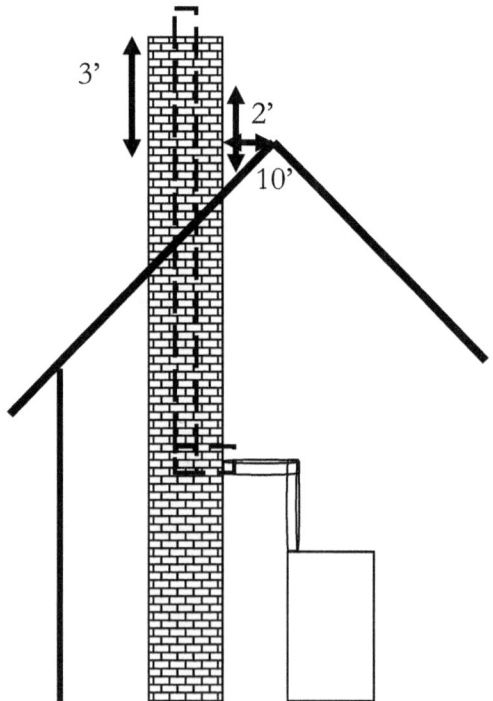

Class A Chimney Installation

You will also need double-wall black stove pipe for the connection from the appliance to the chimney wall thimble.

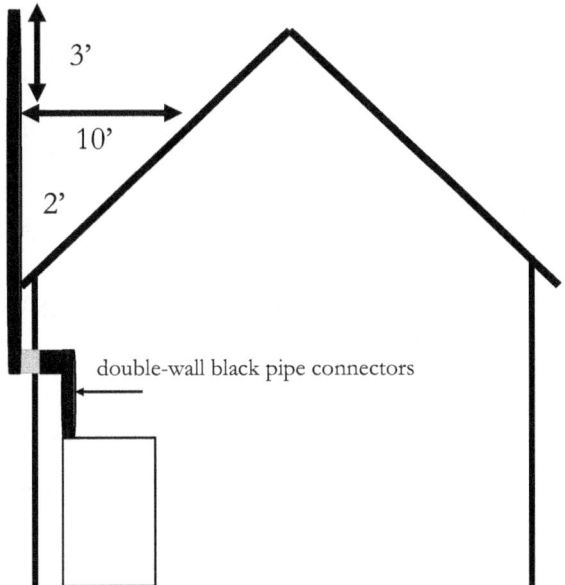

Note: If the installation is not done by a professional CSIA Certified Chimney Sweep or NFI Certified Woodburning specialist your insurance company may withdraw coverage.

3'

10'

2'

double-wall black pipe connectors

Class A Chimneys

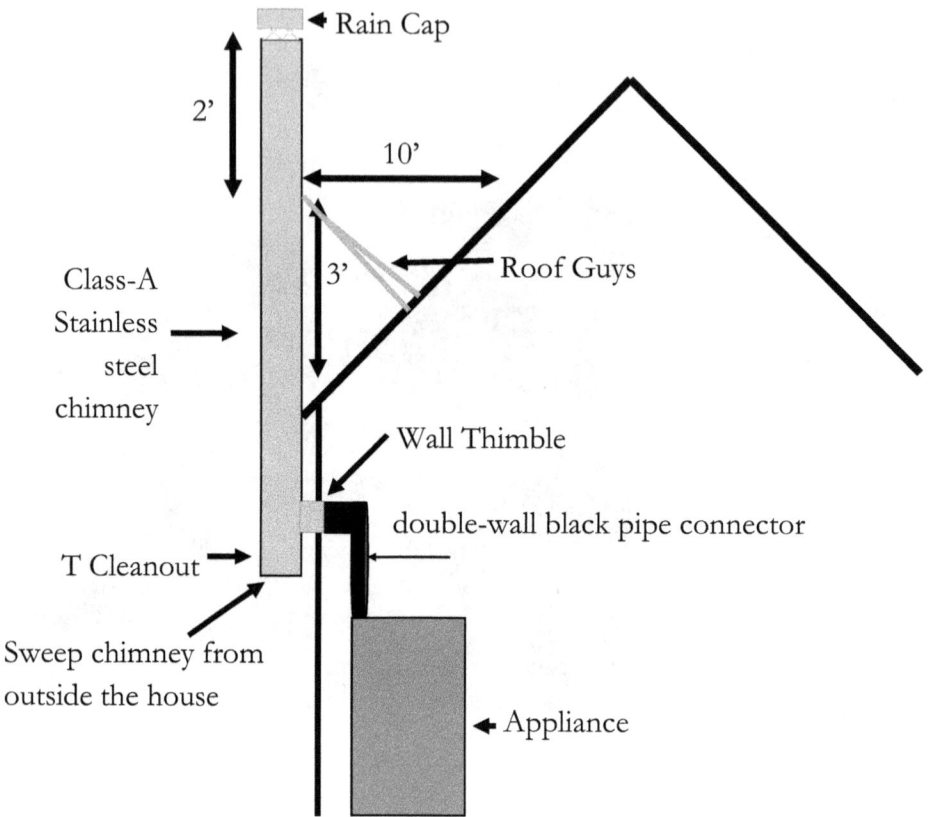

Rain Cap

2'

10'

3' ← Roof Guys

Class-A
Stainless →
steel
chimney

Wall Thimble

double-wall black pipe connector

T Cleanout →

Sweep chimney from
outside the house

← Appliance

CLASS A CHIMNEY INSTALLATION

A Class A chimney is not a flue—it is a chimney and flue in one. This is a U.L. Listed and tested chimney system that consists of a double-wall stainless steel chimney with insulation packed between the walls. There are several components that may come with it depending on your particular needs including, the pipe, a wall thimble, flashing, rain cap, clean out T, and guy supports if needed. You will also need double-wall black stove pipe for the connection from the appliance to the chimney wall thimble. Class A chimney pipe is not cheap, so expect to pay even more than the appliance cost. This is definitely NOT a DIY project so be sure to hire a professional to do the job. If clearances are not adhered to or something is installed incorrectly it can be a severe fire hazard.

How to Find a Qualified Chimney Sweep

Finding a qualified chimney sweep to inspect or sweep a chimney may be more difficult than most people think. Unlike Heating, Ventilating and Cooling Technicians, chimney sweeps are not required to have any training or licensing in most jurisdictions when performing sweeping or inspection services. Only a few states, counties, and cities require chimney sweep licensing.

Some cities like Topeka, Kansas; Columbia, Missouri; and Des Moines, Iowa do require that a chimney sweep have certification from the Chimney

Photo: adobestock.com

Safety Institute of America, but in most towns homeowners are left to their own devices to determine if the company they hire is actually qualified to do the work.

Unfortunately, the Midwest Chimney Safety Council has received a large number of complaints from consumers who have received bad advice or service from untrained chimney companies. But there is little that the MCSC can do about such complaints if the company is not a member for example, no discipline can be rendered.

One new Kansas City, Missouri homeowner was given ill advice when a chimney sweep told her that here wood-burning stove insert, which was installed a wood chimney chase, was safe to use. The sweep had used a dental mirror to do an inspection of the flue. A second inspection from a qualified company revealed the wood chase and the severe fire hazard and code violation.

In yet another case an Overland Park, Kansas resident was shocked to hear that flue liners recently installed were the wrong size, and that they were causing smoke backup from the fireplace and Carbon Monoxide backup from the water heater and furnace flue. The family had been ill with flu-like symptoms which went away after they left the house. The installer had no credentials, but the homeowner assumed he did since he had a business license.

Although no license may required for chimney sweeping or inspections, homeowners can make sure that the chimney sweep is certified by the Chimney Safety Institute by visiting their website at www.csia.org.

Also check the company website for length of time in business, other related certifications, and samples of the company's work. A call to the Better Business Bureau may reveal interesting facts as well but keep in mind that most people don't report problems to the BBB.

Chimney sweeps deal with fire in people's homes. If the sweep doesn't know the NFPA 211 Standards or International Residential Code requirements such as clearances to combustibles or proper chimney construction, he or she can put the homeowners at risk simply by being ignorant of the information.

Doing the job of chimney sweeping is critical – if it is not done correctly the risk of fire can be greater than if the flue were never touched. Surprisingly, some untrained chimney sweeps don't have the proper equipment to do the job correctly. They sometimes sweep out the flue and leave creosote on the smoke shelf where it is closer to the fire. Creosote is very flammable and can ignite if a spark or flame touches it. By not sweeping out and vacuuming the smoke shelf a worse fire hazard is created. For this and other reasons, homeowners should be very careful about who they hire for this important job.

According to the National Fire Protection Association, over 15,000 fires occur annually due to improper chimney, fireplace, or wood-burning stove maintenance or installation.

City codes require licensing of plumbers, electricians, HVAC technicians, contractors, and beauticians in the interest of public safety, so why not license chimney technicians who deal with fire and carbon monoxide in peoples homes? That question can only be answered by the states and county codes officials.

Things homeowners should know:

♦ A business license is not a contractor license. Anyone can get one.

♦ There is no license required to be a chimney sweep or chimney inspector in most jurisdictions (with a few exceptions).

♦ Some jurisdictions require A CLASS DM or HVAC contractor license to install flue liners or hearth appliances Some also requires an HVAC supervisor license. Check with your local building code department for more information.

♦ The only nationally recognized chimney sweep training and certification program is through the
Chimney Safety Institute of America. Visit the CSIA website at www.csia.org for more information and to find a qualified chimney sweep near you.

Tips for finding qualified chimney sweep:

♦ See if the sweep is CSIA Certified (www.csia.org)

- Check their website to see what services they offer and if it looks professional

- Ask how long they have been in business

- Ask for a copy of their worker's Comp and Liability insurance certificate

- Check their references

- Ask for referrals from your friends and neighbors

Health Benefits of Fire and Wood

The following are articles from our Wood-Fired Heating and Cooking blog and Wood-Fired Magazine

Health Benefits of a Fire in the Hearth

By Alice Brink

What is it about a fire in the fireplace that immediately elicits feelings of comfort and ease? Is it the warmth, the sound of gentle crackle and pop, the rhythmic pattern of undulating flames…?

Perhaps all three; along with the added benefit that a fire invites us to slow down, *sit* down, and enjoy it.

Our modern lifestyle can keep us in a constant state of high alert status, or the "fight, freeze or flight response." (FFF) This is a normal, healthy response to stimulus or threat that has kept us humans on the planet for millennia. A tiny, 2-part gland called the Amygdala that rests in the center of our brains is programed to keep us safe by remembering a threat and triggering a response to it. IE: Stimulus = Saber-toothed Tiger, Response = Fight, Freeze or Flight.

However, that ancient protective response can be triggered by not-so-life -threatening stimulus in our world today. In its effort to make sense of the stimuli that it is constantly bombarded with, the Amygdala can generalize and lump vaguely similar threats together. Think about your most recent trip on a highway. Did someone cut you off?, not let you in traffic?, run a stop sign? (and you had your kids in the car- whew!) Your Amygdala reads those stimuli in exactly the same way it has been programmed to read "Saber-toothed tiger" – Yikes! In addition, the sub-conscious does not know the difference between "real" and "virtual," so even violent or disconcerting images on TV and through other media can prompt the FFF response.

That protective response floods the body with adrenaline, increases heart rate, slows digestion, tenses muscles and pumps blood to the extremities for fight or flight, leaving the brain sorely lacking in the nourishment it needs for optimal function and us feeling like we just ran a marathon. No wonder we are tired after a long day!

Fire in the hearth Photo: Adobestock.com

A surprisingly simple, comforting and elegant way to de-stress and sooth the FFF response is to enjoy the benefits a fire in the hearth.

Raising body temperature just a few degrees allows more efficient circulation; relaxing the muscles and bringing essential nutrients and oxygen to all parts of the body; creating a feeling of safety, security and ease.

The sound of the gentle sizzle and crackle of the burning wood serve as pleasant "white noise" which gives the brain just enough to occupy it, allowing other over-stimulated parts (ie: the Amygdala) to relax and rejuvenate

The almost hypnotic visual pattern created by dancing flames also serves as a pleasant pre-occupation for an over-stimulated brain and may even induce an Alpha brainwave response similar to that experienced in meditation or hypnosis.

Maybe our ancestors were on to something. After a hard day in Saber-tooth-ville- Fire Good Medicine.

Alice Brink is a Self-Empowerment Coach, Trainer and Mind/Body Healthcare Practitioner and may be reached at www.alicebrink.com

Chopping Therapy

By Audrey Elder

Photo: adobestock.com

That's right, chopping therapy. Me, a nice warm red and black flannel, my hiking boots, my axe and wedge. Out to the woodpile I go, find a nice wide chunk of walnut, lift the axe up over my right shoulder…. and whack! I remember why I brought the wedge. Either way, after a full wheelbarrow load of fresh split logs for the fire… I feel better.

Full disclosure here, I own a gas-powered log splitter. That's not the point. There are just those moments in life that require a break from everything, a little exercise induced endorphins and a zoned in focus on a simple task. For me, there is no better way to achieve this than chopping firewood.

Imagine this scenario. It's a beautiful chilly Saturday in October. A crisp cool north wind pours across the yard carrying hundreds of gold and red leaves from summers fading trees with each gust. Inside, a full house filled with the sounds of individual activity. *Kerplunk, boink, swoosh, boink,* ahh someone is playing a game on their tablet. Someone else is having a lively conversation on their phone. Another is cranking up the volume on the television, this is their favorite part of the movie! You clutch the book in your hand, your eyes roll slightly, the plot has just begun to reveal itself. You count to ten. The words blur as if they refuse to be legible amongst ALL THE NOISE. See? This, this my friends, is when the woodpile calls to save your sanity.

 It could be a needed break from a frustrating event like trying to put a dresser together that came in a flat box. It could be when your computer decides to update everything the moment you're about to send the email that was due an hour ago. Or, in 2020, it could just be because it's 2020. Whatever it is that brings you to the brink of allowing your inner five-year-old who didn't get a puppy to show up around any other human, nothing works better than chopping therapy. Not to mention the added bonus of never having to leave your home, spending NOTHING, and actually getting something accomplished.

The first log that splits all the way through creates an inner celebration. A joy of nearly primal accomplishment. There I stand above my TWO pieces of firewood holding my axe to the sky, steam pouring from each breath into the frigid air as I think about how this act may please my flannel wearing ancestors who chopped wood or froze. Depending on what level of angst brought me to this place, I may keep chopping!

I might look down at those two pieces of firewood and think, *those are a bit large.* I might decide to split each of them as well. I of course negate the wedge with at least the first whack. Even this will provide a place to pound the wedge in. The first piece splits! Ah Yes! I am still dominating this wood pile! The second piece….whack…wedge….whack….wedge stuck…whack….wedge stuck further….wood turned sideways….attempt to push wedge out with axe…axe is stuck….lift axe with log attached and beat log on another log… At this point, whatever has brought me to this place is gone and forgotten. It's just me and the impossible piece of wood. It's war and I'm determined to win.

So, whether I actually do win and leave pushing my wheelbarrow full of firewood pridefully to the front porch or I end up having the emotional outbreak I likely needed to in the first place, its over. I'm ready to return to the task inside that awaits me. Refreshed, clear headed and completely physically exhausted.*

These kinds of days end the same way all days do, the sun goes down. We all gather in the living room after dinner to watch a show, cozy and warm as the fire flickers through the glass door of the woodstove. My husband lovingly reaches over and taps my shoulder, "You look like you feel much better now." I smile with tranquility, "I do feel better dear, much better."

Chop safely, chop often, and always chop for inner peace. In some odd way, I'm sure this helps make the world a better place.

*For the same results in the summertime, spend half an hour trying to start a gas-powered lawnmower.

"Wood warms you twice ...once when you cut it and again when you burn it."

Henry Thoreau

Far Infrared Heat Health Benefits

By Marge Padgitt

W ood-fired appliances produce far infrared rays (FIRs), which are a part of the light spectrum that are invisible to the naked eye. FIRs have the ability to penetrate deeply in to the skin and body tissues and when this occurs cellular vibration speeds up, thereby creating internal body heat.

This not only feels good, but improves health as well. It is also why you will always find your dog or cat lying in front of your wood-fired appliance.

Persons with arthritis, fibromyalgia, or who have muscle or tissue damage benefit from radiant heat. In Europe, some masonry heaters were built with beds connected to the side under the heat channels so that the older generation could receive the benefits of this heat.

But that is not all - the effects of radiant heat cause blood vessels and capillaries to dilate. This increases circulation and removes metabolic waste and toxins through sweating. The heat increases energy production of cells, raising the metabolic rate.

Radiant heat does not heat the air directly, the radiation warms the solid surfaces in the room and will even pass through walls.

Another benefit of using a radiant heating appliance is the reduction of dust in the air caused by forced-air heating appliances. This can reduce throat and skin dryness in the winter months.

Not all FIR producing heating appliances produce the same amount of heat, however. The difference is not only in the type of appliance being used but also the type of material on the exterior "skin" of the appliance.

By far, soapstone is considered by many professionals to be the best material not only because it is beautiful, but because soapstone holds twice as much heat per pound as iron or steel. Soapstone holds heat longer, and releases it over a longer period of time.

Due to the qualities of soapstone, it is a popular choice for masonry heaters, and due to the construction style of a masonry heater, a load of wood will heat the home for a longer period of time than a wood stove. There are also some wood stoves that have an exterior soapstone shell - Hearthstone is one such brand.

ELECTROMAGNETIC SPECTRUM

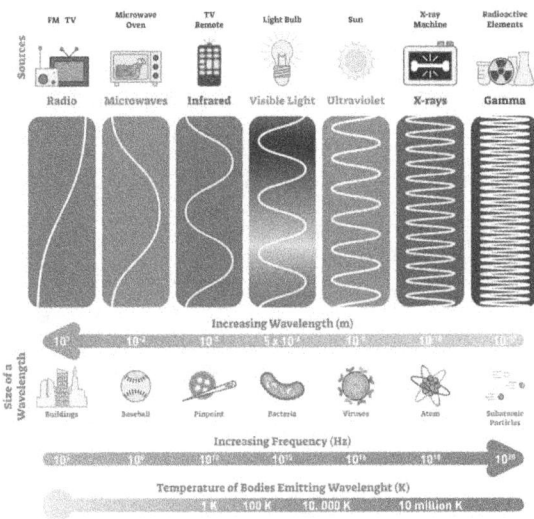

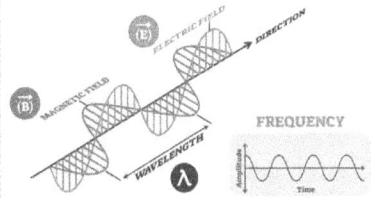

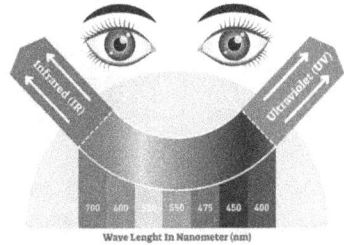

Chapter 4
Wood-Fired Cooking Appliances

There are basically five options for cooking with wood as the fuel. Let's start by saying that once you cook in a wood-fired oven you'll never go back to gas or electric. That is because the flavor can't be beat. So for some this might be the first option, rather than an emergency-only option. In this chapter we will cover the following:

- Use the top of a wood-fired heating stove
- Install a wood-fired cook stove with range and oven inside the house
- Cook on an open campfire, grill, or smoker outside
- Use an indoor or outdoor masonry oven (brick or precast) for cooking and baking
- Use an outdoor cob oven for cooking and baking
- The Tandoor Oven

Each of these options has its pros and cons, and obviously, different price ranges. If you have a cabin somewhere as a getaway retreat, these could be a good option for cooking as well.

The same rules for selecting wood and storing wood apply for cooking as they do for heating, except that you may wish to add a collection of apple, cherry, or other types of flavored woods to use for smoking.

Option A: Use the top of a heating stove

Some freestanding stoves and hearth stoves are set up with a stainless steel cooktop for this purpose, but you can cook on top of a steel or cast iron stove anytime. Most people use trivets when to there is no stainless cooktop in order to protect the finish. This is practical for a one or two person household, or for emergencies of short duration, but not very practical for larger families or long-term electrical outages.

The stove top will get very hot, enough to simmer water, but it may take a bit longer to cook food than a gas range would. And there is obviously no oven. There are some cast-iron skillet recipes available that include all types of foods including breads and cakes that can be cooked on top of the stove. *Tip: Get an electronics charger to attach to the stovepipe. This will provide enough electricity to power a light bulb or charge your cell phone.*

Old 1930's photo source: Adobestock.com

Option B– Use a Cookstove

Wood-burning cookstoves have been around for a long time, we can thank Count Rumford for this as well, going back 200 years. Although you may picture people using them routinely in the 19th Century and early 20th century, they are equally as good today, and stove manufacturers still make them. We know of one person who is in her 90's and still lives at home using her 1860's cookstove handed down through the generations, and she won't consider switching to gas. She loves her wood cookstove.

These stoves can serve as double-duty for heating as well, so are especially suited for cabins or for emergency heating purposes, or as an extra stove on a lower level of the house. The only drawback is that in the summer it will get hot in the room its in! The old-times had a separated space for the kitchen just to keep the heat out of the main house in summer months.

Count Rumford invented the Rumford range which was a brick firebox with an iron top and registers to control heat. His genius idea was a flat top with round ports of different sizes which opened to the fire below, into which the cook would lower pots and pans. In the 19th century the advent of cast iron made making cookstoves much easier—and they could be shipped anywhere. Many of these stoves were purchased through the Sears and Roe-

Left: Lincoln family wood fired stove in the kitchen of the Springfield Lincoln home, Illinois. Author User:Dschwen | Daniel

131

Wood-Fired Heating and Cooking

A resurgence in homesteading and self-reliance has kick-started the use of wood-burning cookstoves. You can find an old refurbished cast-iron stove, buy a new cast-iron cookstove, or have a mason build a cook stove complete with an oven out of masonry and finish the exterior with brick, stone, tile, kachelofen, or soapstone.

Cook stoves also provide heating, so one appliance may be all that is needed.

Jessica Steinhäuser, owner of StoneHouse Kachelofen in Guelph, Ontario, Canada
(https://shko.ca/), built this cook stove with custom multi-shaded vibrant red Kachelen ceramic tiles and stainless steel hardware.

Dean Palmer Photography, Guelph, Canada

Outdoor Brick Ovens

This is a barrel-arch oven that Gene built in our backyard. Lower right: Gene is constructing the arch portion using forms he cut out of heavy duty construction foam. Fresh herbs from the herb garden he built to match always go on our pizzas and in other foods.

Outdoor brick oven in Kansas City

Gene added travertine tile to extend the patio area of the client's home, then built this brick oven using bricks and the same Flemish bond pattern as the house. He added a slate tile roof so it would look like it had always been a part of the original design. These home-owners use the oven quite often when entertaining. Note that the pizza peels are hanging on the right side of the oven for quick access. Racks are made for this purpose. A wood bin is often placed under ovens to keep wood dry and ready for use.

An outdoor brick oven in Independence, Missouri that Gene built. This is at one of our short-term rental houses and we advertise it as a chef's cottage. There is an herb garden on the patio, and Gene has plans to built a counter to the right of the oven with a barbecue. Photo: HearthMasters, Inc.

Tandoori Ovens

I was first introduced to Tandoor ovens during a trip to the U.K. in 2005 with my husband, Gene, and Martin Glynn, a chimney sweep and friend who lives near London. Martin took us to an Indian restaurant and were so impressed with the food we asked what type of oven they used. The surprised waiter was more than happy to take me back to the kitchen where I got to see the oven at work with hot coals in the bottom of a clay oven and meat cooking inside. A few years later we watched a Tandoor oven being built out of firebrick at a Masonry Heater Association workshop. It was at that point I decided that we needed to have our own Tandoor oven in our back yard – something I'm still trying to convince Gene to build.

Tandoor ovens are more commonly used in India, some regions of central Asia, and Arabic countries, but are becoming more popular in the U.S. and U.K. Unlike traditional ovens with a door on the front, Tandoor ovens are cylindrical or egg-shaped with the opening at the top.

Clay pots and assembly By Kamtrewal (Own work) [CC BY-SA 3.0 (http://creativecommons.org/licenses/by-sa/3.0)], via Wikimedia Commons

Food is normally placed on long skewers, which are then placed inside the oven for cooking.

Traditional flatbread is cooked on the sides of a tandoor– the cook shapes the dough, then throws it on the side of the oven where it sticks and cooks.

Tandoors are usually made out of bricks or clay and fueled with wood or charcoal to reach temperatures upwards of 900

Fahrenheit. Food normally cooks very quickly via convection, conduction, and radiation. The temperature can be controlled by the cook via the amount of fuel burned. It is common for tandoors to remain lit by leaving coals in side the oven during cooking to maintain higher temperatures.

One of the most popular dishes prepared is Tandoori Chicken. This excellent dish is chicken roasted with yogurt and spices. The chicken is first marinated in yogurt and honey and seasoned with tandoori masala spice mixture which contains red chili powder, cayenne pepper, turmeric, and paprika. The spice combinations give the chicken its bright red color. This dish is reported to have been invented in 1947 by Kundan Lai Gujral, a restaurant owner in Delhi. Tandoori chicken is also used as a base ingredient in Indian curries and traditionally served (an Indian flatbread). The dish is now served in Britain as Chicken Tikka Masala.

If the Tandoor bug has bitten you, there are ovens available for purchase (check the internet) or build one yourself. I found some plans that don't look too difficult on instructables.com and lifehacker.com, and even some videos on You Tube. The idea is too have heat coming from all sides so the food cooks fast and evenly.

DIY projects are constructed using a metal trash can (no galvanized) or large terra cotta pot with a smaller terra cotta pot inside of it with vermiculite insulation poured between the two pots. Some builders even use firebrick at the base.

These ovens are not as heavy duty as the commercial ovens, but according to the builders/cooks they work fine for home use in the back yard. High temperatures can be reached, and the food cooked in them is delicious.

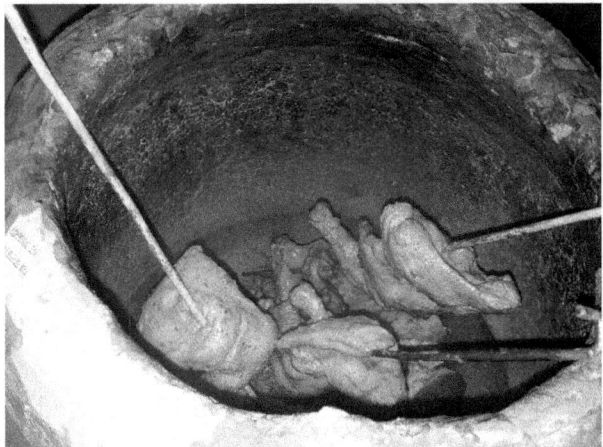

Chicken cooking in a clay tandoor oven

DIY—Plant Pot Tandoor Oven

By Andrew Truran (reprinted from Wood-Fired Magazine issue #7)

This is a quick and easy way to make your own backyard Tandoor oven that can reach temperatures over 400 degrees using readily available materials from you local hardware store.

Step 1: Setup

You'll need three unglazed terracotta pots, one large (approximately 18"), one medium (approximately 11") and one small (approximately 9"), and one cubic foot of vermiculite and pumice if desired. (pumice is optional but makes a nice finished look)

Step 2: Prep

Cut the bottom off of the middle and small sized pots with a masonry grinder. Use electrical tape to mark a line and cut along the center of the tape to prevent cracked edges.

Step 3: Insulation

Place the large pot on bricks, leaving the center bottom hole unobstructed. Place the small pot upright in the large pot so holes line up. If using pumice, make two cardboard cones that are 2" larger than the pots to place around the interior pots. If using pumice, pour vermiculite between the pots and the cardboard, then pour pumice around the cardboard. Otherwise, use vermiculite to fill the space completely. Leave the top 12" unfilled. Remove the cardboard cone. Wear a face mask and gloves when pouring the vermiculite.

Step 4: Assembly

Place the mid sized pot's large opening down on top of the small pot and continue filling the void as before either with or without the cardboard cone.

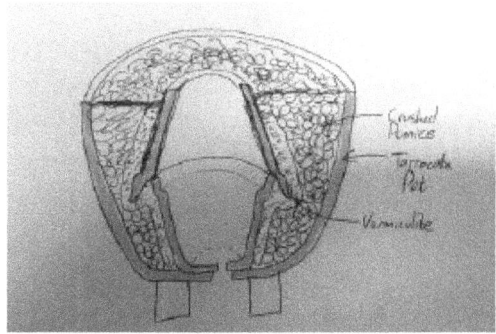

Step 5: Finishing.

Use a layer of pumice to finish the top. Remove the second cardboard cone.

Step 6: First firing

For the first burn do not cook anything in the oven. Use clean burning fuel like charcoal so it doesn't create too much smoke. Keep a fire in the oven for 4– 6 hours to test and prepare the cooking surface. Once fully cooled, give the inside cooking surface a clean with salty water. This helps prepare the surface for nann flatbreads.

Step 7: Nann cooking

Use your favorite naan recipe and apply each nan to the inside of the hot tandoor oven. I used a wet glove to handle the bread. Spray bread with water before applying and it wont burn.

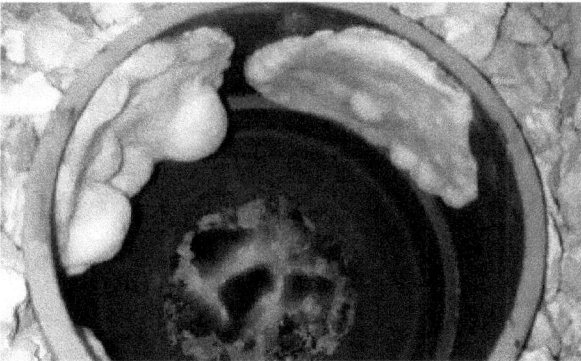

Nann flatbread cooking in a tandoor oven

Photos: Andrew Truran

About the author: Following a Masters degree in Aeronautical Engineering, Andrew worked as a performance and systems engineer for Cobham Mission Systems. During this time he became a chartered engineer and I maintain my CEng status through the Sydney branch of the Royal Aeronautical Society. For the last two and a half years I have been working for Pentair Valves and

Indoor Barbecue Turned Oven

One of our customers wanted to turn an old unused indoor barbeque grill into a small brick oven. We first built a landing support, then a fire-brick oven which was covered with ceramic wool insulation, then finished the exterior. The oven is the perfect size for a pizza, loaf of bread, chicken, or casserole. The customer uses it on a regular basis.

Note: This is a "Black Oven" (fire is built right inside the oven)

Indoor barbecues were popular features in 1970's homes. If you have one of these and don't use it, consider changing it to an indoor oven, which is for some, a more practical application.

Added support for the landing

Installing firebrick

Ceramic wool insulation is used to keep heat inside the oven.

Finished project with a cast-iron oven door and stone landing area.

Photos by Gene Padgitt

How to Make Your Own Charcoal for Outdoor Cooking

By Alan Daugherty

Note: This article originally appeared as "Charcoal Selfie" in issues 6 of Wood-Fired Magazine.

Charcoal purchases for that type of grilling could become a thing of the past. It is certainly not by need, or accident, that one home grill chef decided that self-made, or home-manufactured, charcoal added to the overall backyard grilling experience. It began with a local source of raw material. A line of Osage orange trees received a power company trimming with the limbs left behind by request.

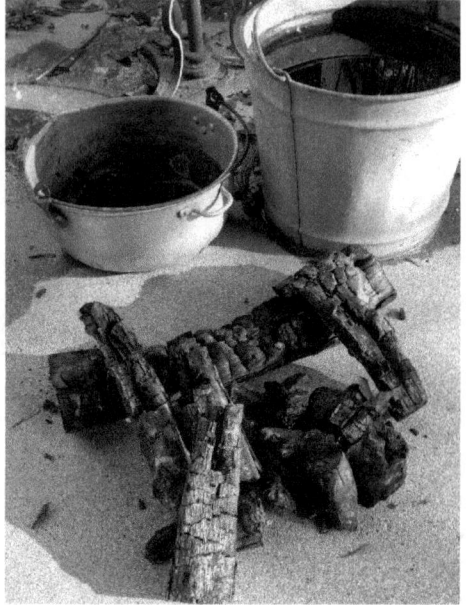

Finished charcoal   Photo by Alan Daughtery

Osage orange (*Maclura pomifera*) trees grow twisted gnarly limbs of wood so hard they can be cut and sometimes use as a replacement for a steel wedge. Identification gets easy in autumn when they begin dropping green grapefruit-size seed balls commonly known as hedge apples. The fruits are inedible to humans, but squirrels love them. The wood can lay rot proof for ages, with the exception of the bark. Unused portions of a stacked cord of Osage orange will last well beyond two decades.

When cut fresh, the heart of the wood is a bright yellow-orange. Trees do not have to be completely cut down for an adequate supply. Limbs of six inch diameter or less provide perfect wood for converting to a barbecue charcoal supply. Cut wood lengths about one foot long, making the

A grove of Osage Orange trees   Photo: Alan Daugherty

firewood pieces right for most wood or charcoal grills.

It is possible with this slow burning firewood, fire consumed at a rate like coal, to provide double duty. A patio firepan or campfire pit fire consisting of Osage orange limbs can be put out with water to salvage the remaining charred wood to be used as charcoal for a grill. A meal of brats cooked over the campfire with hot dog forks can be followed by another day's charcoal grill meal of filet mignon and asparagus; all cooked using the same wood. Osage orange is a win-win.

Charcoal creation is as easy as lighting a small wood fire. Once the long chunks have burned on the outside for twenty to thirty minutes, dip them in a bucket of water and set aside to dry. Use long heavy tongs and a grill glove while working with hot logs. What's left is usable charcoal. Selfie charcoal. Remember to make s'mores while home-manufacturing the Osage charcoal.

Creating one's own homemade charcoal is a bit over-the-top for the traditional family accustomed to burned skin hotdogs or flash-fire burgers on the occasional Saturday afternoon. However, if one gets serious about trying new things while getting back to basics with smokers and charcoal grills, then going beyond selfie rub recipes might just be selfie charcoal. Sure, other woods like hickory and oak would work, but the same chunks of Osage orange charcoal have been known to be snuffed out after use in a Weber Kettle Grill and then relighted for a new day of barbecuing up to five times. Neighbors might think you a bit on the eccentric side when word gets around that you manufacture personalized charcoal, but the self-satisfaction is huge.

Osage orange can often be found growing in a row of considerable length, rather than an isolated tree among other varieties in a forest. Osage orange limb's rot-resistance has long been known. Back as far as the middle 1800s the limbs were used as fence posts. Other farmers planted Osage spaced close together forming a natural, interlocking, thorny, hedge to keep livestock in a pasture, or wild animals out of growing crops. In many places those rows of Osage took root and continue to grow today. Thinning a few trees for a load of firewood will not harm the tree, or the beauty of the rural column of aged stalwart sentinels. Trunks are best left undisturbed due to the fact that most will have wire fencing or barbed wire embedded in the wood. They began as a fence post but soon took root. One such line of trees where one tree was cut to ground level proved to be over 150 years old by counting the rings in the yellow stump.

Native Americans used the flexible but super strength Osage wood for clubs and bows. The tree grew naturally in the area where the Osage Native American tribe lived, hence the tree's common name origin. That with the fact the hedge apple fruits do have a tinge of citric aroma. The debate has long continued as to the spider and insect deterrent quality of the hedge apples. The long hard thorns of the Osage tree may have even been used by pioneer or Native Americans as needles, leather hole punches, or nature's wooden toothpicks.

If anyone decides to try Osage orange wood for homemade charcoal, do keep in mind the tree variety is declining rapidly. They have been found in over two-thirds of the states, but remain most prolific in the Great Lakes and Midwest states. Do not kill the Osage orange tree by over-cutting, or clear-cutting. Allow it to produce and likely after you have secured and used all you need for many years, the tree will have produced that much again on new limbs.

Once you have gone to all the trouble of creating your own supply of charcoal from the Osage orange wood, do not waste it on hot dogs. Grilling a nice filet mignon is no more expensive than going out to eat at a steakhouse. Grilling it right, at home, using your own wood-to-charcoal ingenuity is well worth the price of top quality meat. Strongly recommended as a grill-cooked veggie supplement to the filet meal are peppers, Vidalia onion, roasting ears, summer squash, whole Roma to-matoes, pre-baked grill-smoked potatoes, and asparagus (to name only a few). Mist all veggies with olive oil.

Sear meat and veggies directly over hot Osage charcoal and then move foods to the opposite side of the grill rack for completing with non-direct heat. Keep the lid down/on as much as possible for that delightful charcoal smoke flavor only real wood can provide. Eat the foods el-natural with only a hint of seasoning, if any at all is needed. Simply enjoy the natural flavors.

Try selfie charcoal one time and you will likely never buy briquettes again. When family and guests pour on the praise for great tasting grilled food, do not forget to inform them about the origin of the heat. Thank a pre-Civil War farmer for planting that Osage orange fence row.

Alan Daugherty is a native Hoosier. He enjoys retirement years from his former teacher and carpenter careers. When not deciding on what next to cook atop his grill, he writes a weekly column, "Angelkeep Journals," published each Thursday in "The News-Banner," the local daily for small town Bluffton, IN. Alan wrote and published books of regional interest that incorporate over 90% true events, but woven together via fictional plots. "Mr. Aarteman's Crayon" and "the FLOOD" remain available on Amazon. Contact Alan at 260.824.8454 or angelkeep@gmail.com

Good Uses for Wood Ash

Instead of throwing ashes away, use them for other projects.

In the Garden:
People have used wood ash in their vegetable and flower gardens for perhaps thousands of years. While tomatoes, fruit trees, bulbs, and root vegetables seem to benefit most, potatoes and acid –loving plants like hydrangeas, azalais, and blueberries will suffer. Use ashes from cord-wood only.

Garden Pest Deterrent: Ashes repel snails and slugs because it dehydrates them. Sprinkle a small amount of ash around the base of your plants to keep these pests away. Re-sprinkle af3er it rains.

Melting Ice: Sprinkle wood ash over ice and watch it melt.

Shining Silver: Try dipping a soft cloth in water, then in ash, and polish your sliver.

Cleaning Glass Doors on Stoves and Fireplaces: Dip a soft cloth in water, then in ash, and scrub the doors. Only do this on cold doors.

How to Re-Season
Cast Iron Skillets

Cast iron skillets are popular among outdoor and indoor chefs. Over-scrubbing cast iron with metal scouring pads can remove the seasoning from your trusty skillet. To restore the finish, use a scrub sponge to remove any rust, clean with a bit of mild dish soap, then rinse and dry well. Place on the stove for a couple of minutes on low heat to thoroughly dry the skillet.

Coat the inside and outside with vegetable oil and bake upside down in the oven at 350 degrees for one hour. Let cool and remove excess grease with a paper towel.

Seasoned skillets will also prevent food from sticking.

Chapter 5
Cooking in a Wood-Fired Oven

Cooking and baking in a wood-fired oven is much different than any other type of appliance, however, anyone can learn how to do it. Brick ovens can stay "at temperature" for long periods of time, which is perfect for baking breads or roasting meats. The trick is getting it to the desired temperature.

Most cooks fire the oven the night before they plan to use it. Firing the oven means putting a fire in it to get it warmed up. There is a lot of masonry mass to heat up with a brick oven, but cob ovens don't take as long to come to temperature because there is less mass.

After using your oven for a while you'll get to know how it works and how much wood to use to heat it, and how to manage it.

Start off by building a small fire in the center of the oven. Let that burn down to coals with the door open. Next, add a few large pieces of wood and get a larger fire going. The oven door will determine how much air gets to the fire, so open or close it as needed to maintain the fire. Close the oven door for the night.

In the morning, re-fire the oven with a load of wood. The amount of wood determines the temperature the oven will reach. After the wood has burned down to coals, push the coals aside to cook pizza so the oven stays very hot. If cooking anything else, remove the coals and use them for your barbecue or put them out.

Use a high-temp thermometer that reaches to 700 degrees F—place it in the oven to check the temperature.

With the temperature at 500—700 degrees it is time to cook pizza! Put corn meal on your pizza peel, place the pizza dough on it and add your ingredients. Do this quickly so the dough does not stick to the peel. Now slip the pizza off the peel directly onto the firebrick floor. Keep an eye on the pizza as it will cook very quickly—in two to four minutes. Turn the pizza as it cooks. When it gets golden brown—almost burned, it is time to take the pizza out of the oven.

When the oven is at 400 degrees F it is time to put bread in for baking. I suggest baking several loaves at a time, and invite your friends neighbors to use the oven for their bread, too. Cook bread right on the oven floor or in a pan. The oven will stay at temperature for quite a while.

Closing the oven door will make it hotter, so if you are losing temperature, close the door, and if it is too hot, open it a bit.

After the oven has dropped to 350 degrees or lower, this is the time to roast a turkey or a couple of big chickens, or roast beef, etc. Do not close the oven door all the way or it will over heat. Add your casseroles, too. Anything will cook in the oven!

When the temp gets down to 250 or below, this is the time to slow-cook meats, or dry herbs. Use the oven as a smoker if you don't have a smoker.

Tip: Add some soaked hickory, apple, or cherry chips to the oven to flavor the food.

Abbreviations:

C or c = Cup

T = Tablespoon

Tbsp = Tablespoon

t = Teaspoon

Tsp = Teaspoon

Lb. = Pound

Pt = Pint

QT = Quart

Recipes for Wood-Fired Ovens

Brick ovens heat using convection and radiation. The food cooks evenly on all sides, so cooking is faster in this type of oven. The bottom gets hotter but by using a rack you'll avoid scorching.

Main Dishes

Perfect Roast Turkey and Gravy

By Gene Padgitt
Tried and tested in our brick oven every Thanksgiving for years—it is the best tasting turkey you'll ever eat!

Ingredients:
1 (18 lb) whole turkey
1/2 cup olive oil
1 tbsp. salt (or to taste)
1 tsp. fresh ground black pepper
1 tbsp. fresh or dried rosemary
1 tbsp. fresh or dried thyme
2 quarts chicken stock
1 cup Blackberry Brandy

Directions:
Heat oven to 325°. If your wood-fired oven is hotter- up to 375° -go ahead and use it. The turkey will brown and cook faster, but it will not dry out.

Thaw turkey and remove the giblets and neck. Rinse the turkey with cool water inside an out then pat dry with a paper towel.

Place the turkey breast side up on a rack in a roasting pan.

In a bowl mix together the olive oil, salt, pepper, thyme, and rosemary then apply to the turkey with a basting brush. Now turn the turkey over so it is breast side down, and season it as well.

Salt the interior cavities. Do not stuff the turkey with dressing– this assures that the bird is cooked thoroughly.

Pour four cups of chicken broth and the brandy in the pan.

Place the pan in the oven on a rack. We use two pieces of angle iron to put the roasting pan on to keep it off of the oven floor and to allow for heat to circulate under the pan.

After an hour or after the turkey is nicely browned, baste the turkey and place an aluminum foil tent over the top to keep the turkey moist. Baste every hour or more often and add more broth to the pan if needed.

Check the internal temperature and roast until the thermometer reads 180 degrees F. The total cooking time may vary based on the temperature of the oven generally about 3 1/2—4 1/2 hours is what we allow for.

Place other dishes (stuffing, sweet potatoes, green been casserole, etc.) in the oven during the last hour of cooking.

Remove turkey and let rest for 15 minutes before carving.

Gravy

Using the same roasting pan with juices, place on a stove top and bring the liquid to a simmer. If there is too much fat or oil skim most of it off. Make a slurry by mixing 4 tbsp. corn starch or flour and water together.

Using a wire whisk, mix the slurry into the pan drippings and stir until hot and bubbly. Add the remaining chicken stock until the gravy is the right consistency. Add two chicken bullion cubes. Stir with a wooden spoon until mixed thoroughly. The brandy gives this gravy a nice flavor.

Brick Oven or Grill Baby Back Ribs

One of our favorite dishes is slow cooked BBQ baby back ribs and smoked in the wood fired brick oven.

Ingredients:
1 rack of baby back ribs
1 Large carrot slices 1/2" thick
1 Large onion
Salt
Pepper
Olive oil
BBQ Sauce
Soaked wood chips, hickory or apple

Directions:
Brick oven is pre-heated to about 200 to 300 F with a small fire

burning in the back.

In a large pot, heat up the olive oil and sear the ribs till brown on both sides. You may need to cut the ribs in half if a full rack so it fits in the pot. Add salt and pepper

As you turn the ribs to sear on the other side add the sliced carrot and onion cut in half so they color as well.

Add water to the pot till the ribs are fully covered. Let it boil for 2 hours.

Remove the ribs from the boiling water and place on a large plate or cookie sheet. Rube the ribs with your BBQ Sauce.

In the brick oven place a grate raised on a couple of brick about 2" from the floor of the oven

Place the wood chips on the coals or fire in the back of the oven

Place the ribs on the grate and close the insulated and cast iron door as well as the damper.

Let the ribs smoke for about 45 to 60 minutes.

Remove the ribs from the brick oven and rub a second time with the BBQ Sauce before serving.

the BBQ Sauce before serving.

A little tip for extra flavor; use the water from the ribs to boil broccoli, carrots or corn. It is full of flavors and would be a waste to not make the most of it.

Baked Lasagna

Ingredients:

One package lasagna noodles, cooked

8 oz. Ricotta cheese

2 cups shredded Mozzarella cheese

2 T fresh basil, chopped

2 C spaghetti sauce (see recipe)

1 lb cooked hamburger or turkey, chopped

1 large onion, chopped

1 T olive oil

1 T minced garlic

2 T parsley

Salt and pepper to taste

Directions:

Heat oven to 350° F.

Cook onion and garlic in a skillet

until the onion is translucent. Spray a 13" x 9" pan with cooking spray. Place the following ingredients in layers in 13x9" oblong pan in order listed, beginning and ending with the sauce. Repeat until all ingredients are used up.

Sauce, single layer of noodles, mixture of : ¾ lb. Ricotta cheese or cottage cheese, 1 tbsp minced parsley, 1 tsp oregano, ¾ c grated parmesan cheese, ¾ lb Mozzarella cheese, grated.

Bake on 350 for 30 minutes. Let stand 15 minutes. Cut into squares and serve with meat balls.

Grilled Chicken Salad Main Dish

Grilled chicken makes for a great salad when mixed with greens and other ingredients. Marinate chicken breasts or thighs overnight in the marinate of your choice depending on the type of salad being made.

This is a great **Lemon Chicken marinade:**

Ingredients:

2 lemons

2 T olive oil

2 t minced garlic

1 T chopped fresh oregano

Salt and pepper to taste

1 1/2 T white wine vinegar

Directions:

Grate lemon rinds, cut lemons in half and save.

Combine all other ingredients in a bowl, add chicken and coat chicken thoroughly, cover with plastic wrap, and leave in refrigerator overnight.

The next day, place the lemon halves on the grill, and grill the chicken on the grill for 5 minutes

Stuffed Bell Peppers
(with or without meat)

by Maria McKenzie

You can omit any meat in this recipe, if desired. To make the meatless version heartier, used canned whole tomatoes. Place one whole tomato into each hollowed pepper and fill the peppers with the rice and cheese.

Ingredients:

(9) med-large multi-colored bell

peppers (ex. green, red, yellow, orange)

Your choice 2 lbs. ground turkey Italian sausage, unseasoned ground turkey, ground beef, or pork Italian sausage)

(2) 5.6 oz. packages Knorr or Lipton Spanish rice

Butter is optional, as instructed on Knorr Lipton package, but I skip in this recipe

4-5 tbsp. Olive oil, if desired

(1) 10-12 oz. can of your preference: diced tomatoes with green chilies or Italian seasoned diced tomatoes

2 cups shredded mozzarella cheese (Tip: Whole or 2% milk fat melts smoother and creamier than skim)

2-3 cups plain tomato sauce

Herbs to taste: Oregano, Basil, Fennel Seed, Thyme, Garlic Salt, Herbs de Provence

Also needed:

Deep dish 13" x 13" casserole pan

Large bowl

Large Skillet

Aluminum Foil

Instructions:

Preheat oven to 375 °F.

Cook rice per instructions on packets, omitting butter, if desired. When done, add olive oil, if desired, and fluff with fork.

Meanwhile, Rinse bell peppers, slice off the tops and core out the centers for filling. Par boil for 6 minutes to partially cook. Be sure to rinse away any seeds.

Brown ground meat thoroughly in a skillet. Season with some or all of the suggested herbs to taste. Once fully cooked and drained, add ½ of the tomato sauce and simmer until sauce is warm.

Pour remaining tomato sauce into the casserole pan covering the bottom.

Arrange peppers (upright) in the casserole pan.

Mix cooked meat and rice in the skillet or a large bowl and stir in the diced tomatoes.

Fill each pepper with a heaping helping of the prepared mixture (some spillage is okay and preferable).

Sprinkle the mozzarella over the peppers.

Loosely cover the peppers with a large piece of aluminum foil and bake until peppers are soft, approximately 40 minutes.

Serve alone or with Italian feast.

Stuffed Pepper Casserole
By Marge Padgitt

Ingredients:

Four green, red, or yellow bell peppers

One medium onion, chopped

16 oz. tomato sauce

1 c rice (optional)

1 lb. ground beef/turkey, or Italian sausage, *or*

1/2 lb. ground beef with 1/2 lb. ground sausage

1 T Fennel seeds

1/4 t salt

1/2 t pepper

Italian seasoning to taste

1/4 c parmesan cheese

8 oz. shredded Mozzarella cheese

Directions:

Cut peppers into two to four slices each depending on size, and place into a pot of boiling water. Parboil for five minutes. Pour 1/4 c sauce on the bottom of a glass pan.

Meanwhile, brown the ground beef or sausage mixed with onion in a skillet with olive oil. Add Fennel seeds, salt, pepper, and Italian seasoning to taste with parmesan cheese (and rice if desired).

Place cooked peppers in the baking pan and cover with the meat mixture and remaining sauce. Top with Mozzarella cheese and bake at 350 °F for 30-40 minutes or until heated through and cheese is melted.

Eggplant Parmesan
By Alice Brink

Ingredients:

One large Eggplant, washed, sliced into ¼ inch rounds and soaked in salt water (teaspoon salt in large bowl). I put a bowl on top of the eggplant to keep it submerged. I leave the skin on.

Heat grapeseed oil in a large skillet.

Dip rounds in flour seasoned with salt and pepper, then in 2 beaten eggs with splash of milk, then Italian bread crumbs mixed with ¼ cup Parmesan cheese. (you can jazz this up to taste with red pepper flakes, garlic powder, etc.)

Fry until golden on both sides— drain on paper towels. Eggplant can be a little firm- will finish in oven.

Sauce:

Sauté ½ large onion in olive oil until translucent.

Add- 2-4 cloves minced garlic to taste

Add- any veggies (carrots, mushrooms, spinach- you want)

4oz tomato paste

1 large can diced tomatoes with juice

Add- 1 teaspoon sugar

Add- 2 tablespoons balsamic vinegar or 1/4 cup wine (one glass for the cook)

Add- 6 +/- fresh basil leaves if you have them, basil paste, or 1 teaspoon dry.

Add- 2 tablespoons mixed Italian seasoning. Simmer until thickened a bit.

Assemble:

Lay the eggplant rounds in a greased 13 x 9 baking dish (I make rows with them overlapping.)

Cover with sauce and 2 cups shredded mozzarella mixed with ½ cup parmesan.

Bake: 350 degrees for 30 minutes.

Veggie Lasagna

By Alice Brink

Use the same sauce from Eggplant Parmesan recipe.

Slice 2-4 zucchini lengthwise thinly to create "noodles"

Prep any veg you like or want to use up! I have used carrots, spinach, onion, tomatoes, olives, kale, peppers- pretty much anything that could lean Italian.

Make ricotta filling with one large (add 2 eggs) or one small (add one egg) container ricotta cheese, depending on whether you make a 9 x 9 or 9 x 13 size pan. Add- salt, pepper, dried parsley, garlic powder to taste.

Assemble- just like regular lasagna, only using zucchini "planks" as noodles.

Top with mozzarella/parmesan shredded cheese mixture.

Bake at 350 degrees for 40 minutes.

Let sit for 20 minutes before serving to set.

Glazed Ham

Score ham by making diagonal slices with a knife. If desired, a whole clove may be inserted in each scored square. This really ads a nice flavor to the ham. Use one of the following glazes and cook ham in a 400 ° F oven for 30 minutes, then cover and cook until done. Use a meat thermometer to check the internal temperature.

Glaze A

1 c brown sugar

1 tbsp dry mustard

½ c pickle juice or spiced fruit juice may be added

Glaze B

1 c brown sugar

¾ c crushed pineapple

Glaze C

1 c cranberry or currant jelly

Easy Chicken Casserole
By Marie Lombardo

Ingredients:

2 lbs. boneless and skinless chicken breast, baked in oven first.

½ stick butter, melted

1 pkg stove top dressing, prepared as directed

1 can cream of chicken soup

1 can cream of celery soup

Enough broth to make fairly moist (add water to broth if necessary)

Directions:

Mix together all ingredients and bake covered in a 9 x 13" dish for 45 minutes at 350° F.

Note: Casseroles are well suited for the wood-fired oven.

Easy & Awesome Chicken Enchiladas
By Celia Reid-Trujillo

Serves 4 – 6

Your guests will think you slaved away (but you didn't) to make these great-tasting enchiladas!

Ingredients:

2 (10-oz) cans green enchilada sauce

1 ¼ c chopped fresh cilantro leaves (IF YOU OMIT this they won't be awesome!)

1/2 c sour cream

1t cumin

1 rotisserie chicken, skin discarded, meat shredded into bite-sized pieces (about 3 c)

2 ½ c shredded cheese (Use what you prefer, i.e., Mexican blend, mild cheddar, cheddar-jack, etc.)

(I think it tastes better if you

shred your own cheese, but if you're short on time or ambition, you don't have to for this recipe) Salt and pepper
12 (6") corn tortillas

Directions:

Adjust oven rack to middle position and heat oven to 400°. Grease 13 x 9" baking dish with cooking spray.

Puree enchilada sauce and 1 cup cilantro in blender. Mix sour cream and cumin together until well blended.

Combine 1 cup enchilada sauce mixture, the sour cream mixture, chicken, and 1½ cups cheese in large bowl and toss to combine. Season with salt and pepper.

Wrap tortillas in clean kitchen towel and microwave until pliable, 30 to 90 seconds.

Top each tortilla with ¼ c chicken mixture and roll tightly (do NOT overfill). Arrange, seam -side down, in prepared baking dish. (Fit 10 side-by-side vertically and 2 horizontally above them) Spray top lightly with cooking spray, then top with additional 1 cup enchilada sauce mixture and remaining cheese.

Bake until cheese is melted and enchiladas are heated through, 15 to 20 minutes.

Sprinkle with remaining cilantro. Serve, passing remaining sauce at table.

These are great served with refried beans and rice (see accompanying recipes) for a complete Tex-Mex meal.

Shepherd's Pie in the Oven

Ingredients:

1 lb ground beef or lamb
1 medium onion, diced
2 cloves minced garlic
10 oz. bag frozen peas and carrots, defrosted or canned peas and carrots, drained
10.5 oz. can of corn, drained
10.5 oz. can of green beans, drained
10 oz. can of tomato or cream of mushroom soup
1 tsp Worcestershire sauce
¼ tsp basil
Dash pepper
3 cups cooked mashed potatoes
1 cup shredded cheddar cheese

Directions:
Preheat oven to 400° F. Cook the ground beef or lamb, onion, and garlic over a stove, grill , or in the

oven. Cook until meat is no longer pink and then drain off the fat. Add in the soup, salt, pepper, basil, and Worcestershire sauce. Spread the meat mixture into the bottom of a 2 quart casserole dish. Sprinkle the carrots, peas, and corn over the meat mixture. Spoon the prepared mashed potatoes over the top. Sprinkle the cheese over the potatoes.

Bake for 25 to 30 minutes or until it is hot and bubbly. *Note: vary the recipe as desired.*

Ham & Swiss Pie

Ingredients:

2 c. cooked ham, cut into 1" cubes
1 c. shredded Swiss cheese
1/3 c. chopped onion
4 eggs
2 c. milk
1 c. Bisquick
¼ tsp salt
¼ tsp pepper

Directions:

Preheat oven to 400 degrees. In a 10" pie plate sprinkle ham, cheese and onions in plate. Beat other ingredients until smooth. Pour into plate and distribute evenly. Bake until golden brown, about 35 to 40 minutes or until knife inserted in center comes out clean. Do not overbake.

Brisket

Ingredients:

1/2 c Brown sugar
1 t Paprika
1 t Onion powder
1 t Garlic powder
1/2 t Cumin
1 t Oregano
Salt and pepper to taste
1 bottle dark beer
1 c vinegar
Brisket

Directions:

Preheat oven to 325 degrees. Mix all ingredients. Rub mixture on brisket on both sides. Put water in the bottom of the drip pan. Baste once an hour for 4 hours. Wrap in foil and cook for 4 hours. Let rest ½ hour before serving.

Pizza

Pizza baked in a wood-fired oven can't be beat. It is by far, the most often cooked food in this type of appliance. Just tell your friends and family that you're having a pizza party and your back yard will be full of people very quickly!

Photo: adobestock.com

Get the oven very hot (500-700 degrees) then put cornmeal on your pizza peel. Place the pizza dough on the peel after shaping it, add your ingredients, then shake the pizza off of the peel and directly onto the oven floor. Turn frequently so it doesn't burn the crust, but a perfect pizza has an almost-burnt crust.

Keep a live fire going too the side to keep the oven piping hot!

We keep an herb garden filled with rosemary, thyme, basil, parsley, and garlic chives just so when people come to visit for a pizza party they can pick herbs of their choice to put on the pizza.

We find that the best way to serve up pizza is to set up a pizza bar with different ingredients and let people help themselves and build their own pizza. Be sure to tell guests not to pile on too many ingredients or the pizza will be soggy and too heavy (good luck with that).

Then Gene cooks all the pizzas while people watch. Serve wine or beer to drink, and a nice fresh salad to go with it. It is great fun for all ages!

Pizza Bar Ingredients:

Pizza dough ready to go

Toppings:
Pepperoni
Ground beef
Ground sausage
Canadian bacon
Cubed chicken
Regular or turkey bacon crumbles
Anchovies
Sliced tomatoes
Thinly sliced onions
Green Peppers
Olives
Pineapple
Banana peppers

Cheeses:
Mozzarella cheese (shredded or sliced)
Parmesan cheese
Romano cheese
Goat cheese

Sauces:
Alfredo
Red pizza sauce
Garlic butter

And don't forget red pepper flakes for those who want to kick it up a notch!

Have cornmeal on hand for the pizza peel!

Why does Pizza taste better when it is cooked in a wood-fired oven?

According to most chefs, wood-burning ovens can do things that gas ovens cannot. Wood-burning ovens can achieve very high temperatures of 700—1,000 degrees, reducing cooking time dramatically. An average 10" pizza will cook in 1 –2 minutes. The pizza will taste fresher and be crisp, like authentic Napolitano pizzas.

The thermal drafts from the wood create a current of air (convection), which allows the food to cook very evenly on all sides. But the most important factor is that the smoke from the wood infuses the crust with flavor that can't be beat.

Once you've tried wood-fired pizza it is unlikely that you will eat any other type again!

White Garlic Sauce for Pizza

By Michael Manahan

Ingredients:

2 T unsalted butter
2 T all-purpose flour
1 1/4 C milk
1/4 t sea salt
1/8 t black pepper
2 garlic cloves pressed or grated
1/4 c shredded parmesan cheese

Directions:

Melt butter in a small saucepan over medium heat. Whisk in flour and continue whisking for 1-2 minutes (do not let it brown) Slowly add milk, whisking constantly until smooth, thickened, and bubbly.
Whisk in salt, pepper, and garlic. Add parmesan cheese and whisk another 30 seconds. Remove from heat and continue whisking just until cheese is melted an sauce is smooth, then set aside to cool before using for pizza. Do not boil after adding cheese or sauce may curdle. Once cool, cover and refrigerate up to 5 days.

Red Pizza Sauce

Ingredients:

1 28 oz can crushed tomatoes
1 T olive oil
2 cloves minced garlic
1 t red wine vinegar
1 t salt
1 t oregano
1/4 t pepper

Mix all ingredients together and use immediately or keep in the refrigerator until needed.

Tangy Ranch Pizza

Instructions:

Make your favorite pizza dough or purchase pre-made dough.

Make buttermilk ranch dressing from a mix. Add two shredded garlic cloves to the dressing. Spread on dough.

Put chicken, green onion, tomato and mozzarella on top of the sauce and bake.

Dessert Pizza

Ingredients:

Pizza dough with 1 t vanilla extract added prior to mixing
1/2 cup brown sugar

1 t cinnamon

1/2 t nutmeg

2 T melted butter

Instructions:

Mix dry ingredients together. Brush melted butter on top of pizza crust. Evenly spread dry ingredients on top and bake until done but not crispy. If desired, add thinly sliced apples or bananas to the top before baking.

Quick Stonefire Pizza With Flatbread

By Maria C. McKenzie

Ingredients:

1 Naan (or other flatbread) (whole), room temperature

1/4 cup Low-fat Shredded Cheese, Italian blend or mozzarella

1/4 cup Baby Portabella Mushrooms, Sliced

1/3 each of Red, Yellow, and Green medium Bell Peppers, or preferred mix of colors

2-3 oz. fully-cooked Grilled Chicken Breast Strips, plain or fajita-style, frozen or thawed

4-5 sprays Olive Oil Cooking Spray or Mist

Ground herbs, if desired, such as Oregano, Basil or Herbs de Provence

Directions:

Slice the veggies and sauté until tender using 2-3 sprays of olive oil from a mister. (Note: If you prefer, you can sauté in drizzled olive oil and/or add a tablespoon of real butter). While this is cooking, warm the chicken in a microwave or cook in another skillet.

Mist the flatbread once or twice with olive oil and sprinkle with herbs if desired. Top with shredded cheese. Once the chicken is ready to eat and the veggies are tender and limp, drain any water or juices and toss together. Top the pizza with the veggie/chicken mixture and bake in your outdoor pizza oven or on a sheet of foil in your oven at 400+ degrees. Pizza is done when the cheese is nicely melted, about 4-6 minutes. Cook longer for crispier crust.

loosely with foil.

Margherita Pizza

This is the most famous pizza in Italy and it has very few ingredients but is delicious!

Make your favorite pizza dough. Put a thin layer of garlic butter sauce on the dough.

Add mozzarella and sliced tomatoes then cook, then add fresh basil leaves and serve.

Dough balls proofing

Marge's Famous "If I tell you I'll have to Kill You" Pizza Dough

Marge created this dough by accident one day when she ran our of all-purpose flour and discovered that it makes a perfect cracker-like crust.

Mix together:
1 1/2 c bread flour
1 1/2 c all-purpose flour
2 T sugar
3 1/2 t instant yeast

Add:
1 1/3 c water
1 T vegetable oil
1 1/2 t salt

Stir well or blend in food proces-

sor. Form into a ball and place in oiled bowl and turn to coat. Place plastic wrap over the bowl and place in proofer or a warm spot until doubled in size.

Heat oven to 500—700 degrees. Cut dough in half or fourths, form in to balls, cover and let rest for 30 to 40 minutes.

When ready to cook, stretch out onto circles or squares. Do not use a rolling pin—use your hands. Flour pizza peel well, place dough on peel and put toppings on immediately, then place in oven. Turn while cooking to keep from burning. Remove when crust is nearly burnt.

For standard pizza dough use all-purpose flour only.

Bread Machine Pizza Dough

Ingredients:

1 C warm water (110°)
2 Tbs. olive oil
1 tsp. salt
3 C unbleached all-purpose flour
1 Tbs. active dry yeast

Directions:

Combine all ingredients in a bread machine pan and run through the cycle. Punch down dough and place on a lightly floured surface. Divide

in half and form into two balls (or divide in fourths for smaller pizzas). Cover with a towel and let rise in a warm place until doubled in size, about 40 minutes.

Stretch in to two 12-inch or four 6-inch pizzas.

Thin and Crispy Pizza Dough for the Bread Machine

Ingredients:

3/4 C warm water
2 cups all-purpose flour
1/2 t salt
1/4 t white sugar
1 t active dry yeast

2 t olive oil

Directions:

Pour water into the bread machine pan, add flour on to of the water, sprinkle with salt and sugar, and top with the yeast. Cycle through the machine. Remove from bread pan and place on a floured surface. (No need to let rise)

Preheat oven to 425°F. Roll or stretch pizza out to 14" inches and place on a pizza baking sheet. Brush the dough with the olive oil.

Bake for 5 minutes, remove and place toppings on the pizza. Return to the oven and bake until desired doneness.

Oven or Grill BBQ Ribs with a Kick
serves 4-6

Rub Ingredients:
3 lbs pork back ribs
1 (8 ounce) jar honey
1 teaspoon paprika
1 teaspoon chili powder
1/2 teaspoon garlic powder
2 tablespoons Old Bay Seasoning
1/2 teaspoon onion powder
1/4 teaspoon celery salt
1/2 cup dark brown sugar
1/4 teaspoon fresh ground pepper
1 medium onion, grated or finely chopped
12 ounces barbecue sauce
1/4 cup white sugar

Directions:
Cut ribs apart and place all ingredients in large roasting pan

Mix together making sure to coat all ribs with this seasonings

Spread ribs out evenly on bottom of pan and cover lightly with foil.

Bake at 375 degrees for approximately 1 hour, turning or stirring occasionally.

You can use broiler for these ribs, just watch more closely, and adjust cooking time. These ribs are also great finished on the grill for a few minutes on each side.

A little tip for extra flavor; use the water from the ribs to boil broccoli, carrots or corn. It is full of flavors and would be a waste to not make the most of it.

Apple-Walnut Chicken Bake
By Marie Lombardo

Ingredients:
1 six oz. pkg. Stuffing mix for chicken
1 Large apple, chopped
1/2 cup raisins
1/2 cup honey Dijon dressing, Divided
1 Cup toasted walnut pieces
6 small boneless skinless chicken breast halves
1/4 Cup shredded cheddar cheese

Directions:
Heat oven to 375° F.

Prepare stuffing as directed in large saucepan. Add nuts, raisins, apples, and 1/4 c dressing, mix.

Spoon into a 13 x 9" baking dish and top with chicken. Brush chicken with remaining dressing. Cover

Bake for 35 minutes, top chicken with cheese, bake 10-15 minutes or until chicken is done.

Side Dishes

Hash Brown Potato Casserole

This is a family favorite, and a perfect dish to cook in the wood-fired oven

24 oz. frozen hash browns (one bag)
2 cups sour cream
1/2 stick butter
1 can cream of chicken soup
1/2 cup chopped green onions
2 cups shredded Cheddar cheese

Directions:
Thaw and drain potatoes. Combine sour cream, soup and butter in a large bowl. Mix well. Add salt, onion and cheese. Blend in potatoes.

Topping: 2 cups crushed potato chips or Corn Flakes mixed with 2 tablespoons melted butter. Spread on top of the potatoes.

Bake uncovered at 350 degrees for about 50 minutes.

Deluxe Green Bean Casserole
By Maria McKenzie

Ingredients:
2 Tbsp. olive oil
1 large yellow onion, sliced thin
2 cans cream of mushroom soup
1 cup milk
8 cans green beans (or fresh green beans)
1 small box fresh mushrooms, sliced thinly
1/4 tsp. ground black pepper
1/4 tsp. sea salt
1 large clove garlic, minced
1 Tbsp. Worcester sauce

Directions:
Heat oven to 350°
Sauté the garlic, onion and mushroom slices in the olive oil until the onion is translucent. Mix the cream of mushroom soup and milk, then add green beans, seasonings, and onion mixture in a large bowl. Place in a large casserole and bake for 30 minutes or until bubbly. Top with French Fried Onion Rings if desired.

Wood-Fired Roasted Corn

In the middle of summer, what best than wood fired brick oven roasted corn! After the oven is nice and hot, pull back the husks and pull out the silky strings, then replace the husks. Put the corn in the oven, husk on to keep it moist inside.

Cook corn in the oven for about 30 minutes and it will be perfectly cooked! Note that the husk will burn but your corn will be roasted to perfection. Or cook on the grill if you prefer.

Oven Roasted Stuffed Tomatoes

Ingredients:

12 large ripe tomatoes. Pepper and Zucchini are great as well

1lbs of ground pork sausage meat (can be replaced with beef or turkey ground meat)

2 large onions diced (should be about 2 cups)

2 fresh eggs

5 garlic cloves, minced

2 cup of fresh bread crumbs, not seasoned

1 tbsp Herbes de Provence

Salt

Pepper

Olive oil

Before starting: With the residual heat of your oven, no fire nor embers- aim for temperature between 400F and 500 F.

Use the insulated door of your oven to retain all the moisture and flavor. This will also allow you to cook at a higher temperature to get lightly caramelized tomatoes and maximum flavor.

A great way to make fantastic fresh bread crumbs is to cut thin slices, about 1/4"thick, of left over bread, and place on a cookie tray in your brick oven. Let them toast until golden or light brown. Simply place in a large bowl and gently crush them with a rolling pin.

Directions:

Rinse the tomatoes. Remove about

1/2" of the top part of the tomatoes, where the stem was attached. Keep those as they will be used to make a lid on top of your stuffed tomatoes

Easy Roasted Veggies

This is one of our favorite dishes, and its fast and easy to make.

Ingredients:

Baby Portobello mushrooms
Vidalia onions
Red, green and yellow bell peppers
Olive oil
Garlic salt
Sea Salt
Fresh ground black pepper
Other herbs as desired/

Directions:

Wash veggies and pat dry. Cut pepper and onion into large pieces 2" wide. Cut onion in wedges. Place veggies on skewers and place on a large glass baking pan to catch oil. Drizzle olive oil over the vegetables, covering all sides. Sprinkle the desired amount of seasoning on the vegetables on all sides, then place in the oven or on the grill for 15—20 minutes or until desired tenderness is reached.

Note: Other vegetables can be substituted.

Roasted Rosemary Potatoes

Ingredients:

6 med-large Yukon gold or red potatoes cut into 1-inch squares
1 large Vidalia onion, chopped
2 tbsp. olive oil
1tbsp paprika
1 teaspoon salt
1/2 teaspoon black pepper
1tbsp dried or fresh rosemary

Directions:

Heat oven to approximately 400 degrees F.

Place all ingredients in a paper bag or large baggie and shake until the potatoes and onions are coated with the seasoning. Place the mixture on a baking pan with sides or in a large glass pan that has been coated with oil. Bake for 30 - 45 minutes.

Deluxe Sweet Potato Casserole to Die For

This can be baked in a cast-iron skillet or baking pan

Ingredients:

2 large cans sweet potatoes
1/2 can frozen orange juice concentrate, defrosted
1 t cinnamon
1 t nutmeg
1 can crushed pineapple
8 oz. chopped walnuts
1/3 cup brown sugar
1 bag small marshmallows

Directions:

Heat oven to 350° F. Place all ingredients except marshmallows in a large mixing bowl and mix together. Transfer mixture to a 13" x 9" baking dish or large cast iron skillet and cover with foil. Cook for 30 minutes. Remove foil and cover the top of the sweet potatoes with the marshmallows, then cook for an additional five to ten minutes or until the marshmallows are browned. Cooks up great in a wood-fired oven!

Zucchini, Squash, and Corn Casserole

Ingredients:

1 large yellow squash, cut in 1/4 inch slices
1 large green zucchini, cut in 1/4 inch slices
3 cups canned corn kernels, drained
1/4 C butter
One large sweet onion, diced
2 cloves minced garlic
6 oz shredded white cheddar cheese
1/2 c sour cream
1/2 c mayonnaise
2 large eggs
Salt and pepper to taste
1 1/2 cups breadcrumbs
1 cup grated asiago cheese

Directions:

Preheat oven to 350°. Place zucchini in a pot of water and boil for five minutes. Drain and dry with paper towels.
Melt 2 T butter in skillet, add

171

onion and sauté until tender. Add garlic and sauté for 2 more minutes.

Stir squash with onions and garlic, 1/2 cup breadcrumbs, cheddar cheese, sour cream, corn, mayonnaise, eggs, salt and pepper and 1/2 c asiago cheese and place into a casserole dish.

Melt remaining butter and stir in remaining 1 c breadcrumbs and 1/2 c Asiago cheese. Sprinkle on top. Bake for 45 - 50 minutes.

Easy Spaghetti Squash Baked in the Oven

Ingredients:

1 large spaghetti squash
2 T butter, diced
1/2 cup brown sugar
1 t cinnamon

Directions:

Cut squash in half and place cut side down in a baking dish with 1 cup water. Bake for 45 - 55 minutes. Remove from oven and place on serving platter, sprinkle with

Oven-Roasted Asparagus

Ingredients:

3 bunches fresh asparagus
2 T olive oil
3 cloves minced garlic
3/4 t salt
1/2 t ground black pepper
1/2 c slivered almonds, toasted (optional)

Directions:

Cut off woody ends of asparagus. Place asparagus in a lightly greased baking sheet with sides. Drizzle olive oil and sprinkle with remaining ingredients except almonds. Bake for 10 minutes at 350°. Transfer to a serving dish and sprinke with almonds.

Corn/Cornbread Casserole

Ingredients:

1/4 C melted butter
2 eggs, beaten
1 can kernel corn, drained
1 can creamed corn
1 8.5 oz package corn muffin mix
8 oz plain yogurt or 1/2 sour cream and 1/2 yogurt

Directions:

Preheat oven to 350°. Combine all ingredients then pour into a 10" cast iron skillet or 8" baking pan coated with cooking spray. Bake for 45 -50 minutes.

Potato Salad

Make ahead of time and refrigerate until needed.

Ingredients

12 medium gold potatoes
10 hard-boiled eggs
4 stalks chopped celery
3 cups mayonnaise
2/3 cup sweet pickle relish
1 cup chopped onion
2 Tbsp vinegar
2 Tbsp mustard (or to taste)
2 tsp Salt
1 tsp pepper
Paprika

Directions

Boil potatoes until done. Meanwhile, chop the celery and onion, then mix all of the remaining ingredients and place in the refrigerator.

Remove potatoes from the pot and let cool. Cut in to 1" cubes, then gently stir into the wet ingredients. Cover with plastic wrap until serving time. Garnish with parsley.

Mashed Potato Casserole

Mix in advance and refrigerate until ready to cook in the oven.

Ingredients:

5 lbs potatoes peeled and cubed
1 8oz carton sour cream
1 8oz pkg. cream cheese
4 tbsp butter
2 tsp onion Salt

Directions:

Cook potatoes in boiling water until tender. Drain and mash. Add remaining ingredients and blend well. Spoon into 9x13 baking dish and cover with aluminum foil. Refrigerate up to 2 or 3 days or freezer. If frozen, defrost one day before baking. When ready to serve bake at 350 degrees for 45 to 60 minutes.

Thanksgiving Stuffing

To go with your turkey cooked in the wood-fired oven

By Alice Brink

Ingredients:

1 stick butter

1 medium onion, chopped

3 stalks celery, chopped

Salt

Pepper

4 cups chicken broth

1 t sage

1 t poultry seasoning

4 cups bread crumbs

1/2 cup raisons

Directions:

Melt 1 stick butter in large skillet, Add 1 med chopped onion and 2-3 stalks chopped celery and cook until onions are translucent.

Add 1 teaspoon sage and 1 teaspoon poultry seasoning, salt and pepper to taste

Add one package bread stuffing and 2-4 cups chicken or turkey broth.

Stir in ½ to 1 cup your choice of: pecans, walnuts, chopped apples, chopped apricots, raisins.

Place in greased 13 x 9 inch pan, cover with foil and bake 350° for 30 minutes, remove foil and bake another 10-15 until nice and crunchy on top!

Harvest Stuffing

Add one pound ground cooked sausage to the stuffing.

Baked Tomatoes

Ingredients:

6 medium tomatoes, chopped

1 small chopped onion

1/2 t salt

2 t sugar

1/8 t pepper

1/2 c Italian bread crumbs

1/2 c parmesan cheese

1 T butter, melted

Directions:

Combine the tomatoes, onion, sugar, salt, and pepper and place in a baking dish coated with cooking spray. Combine the remaining ingredients and sprinkle over the tomato mixture.

Bake, uncovered at 350° for 25-30 minutes.

Breads

Old Fashioned Southern Biscuits

For the wood-fired oven

Ingredients:

2 cups (10 ounces) all-purpose flour

1 tablespoon baking powder

1/4 teaspoon baking soda

3/4 teaspoon kosher salt

3 tablespoons (1-1/2 ounces) unsalted butter, chilled, cut into 1/2-inch cubes

3 tablespoons (1-1/4 ounces) vegetable shortening, chilled, cut into 1/2-inch cubes

1 cup buttermilk

Directions:

1. Preheat oven to 450 degrees F.

2. In a medium-size bowl, whisk the flour, baking powder, baking soda, and salt together to blend. The mixture should be light and free of lumps.

3. Add the butter and the shortening, and toss gently to coat. Cut in with a steel cutter until the butter pieces are pea-size.

4. Add the buttermilk all at once.

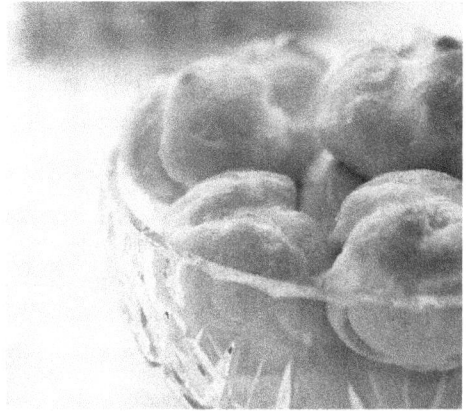

With a wooden spoon or rubber spatula, mix the ingredients until they're just blended and coming together to form a dough. Do not overmix. Overmixing will cause the biscuits to be dense.

5. Empty the dough onto a well-floured work surface. Gently pat the dough out into a rectangle measuring approximately 12 x 8 inches. Lightly flour the surface of the dough. Fold the dough into thirds, as if you are folding a letter. Scrape the folded dough from the work surface; if necessary, flour the surface again. Once more, pat the dough into a rectangle, flour lightly, and fold into thirds. Finally, pat the dough out to a thickness of approximately 1 inch.

6. With a well-floured 2- or 2-1/2-inch round biscuit cutter, cut bis-

cuits out, and place them on a baking sheet. You may reshape biscuits from the scraps, but they will not rise as high as the first cutting.

7. Bake for 12 to 15 minutes, or until the biscuits are a light, golden brown. If you would like, biscuits can be brushed with an additional coating of melted butter. Serve immediately. Homemade biscuits are best eaten the same day that they are baked, but any leftovers can be eaten warm the next day.

Almond Poppyseed Muffins
By Marie Lombardo

Ingredients:

4 large eggs
½ tsp salt
2 c sugar
4 c flour
13 oz can evaporated milk
1 tsp vanilla extract
¼ c milk
1 tsp almond
2 c vegetable oil
½ c poppy seeds
3 ½ tsp baking powder

Directions:

Preheat oven to 325 degrees. Line 30 muffin cups/papers. Beat eggs, sugar, milk, evaporated milk and oil. Sift together flour, baking powder and salt. Gradually add flour to egg. Add flavors and seeds. Mix together until blended. Use 1/3 c to fill cups. Bake for 25-30 minutes.

Egg Bread

Measure into mixing bowl;
1/2 c warm water (not hot)

Add, stirring to dissolve...
2 pkg active dry yeast.

Stir in;
1 ½ c lukewarm milk
¼ c sugar
1 tbsp salt
3 eggs
¼ c soft butter
Half of 7 ¼ to 7 ½ c sifted flour

Directions:

Mix with spoon until smooth. Add enough remaining flour to handle easily; mix with hand. Turn onto lightly floured board;

knead for 10 minutes or until smooth. Let rise in a large oil-coated and covered bowl until double in size. Keep the bowl in a warm place.

Divide the dough into three equal parts. Shape each section into a long rope the length of a cookie sheet. Braid the bread on the cookie sheet.

Preheat oven to 425 degrees. Let dough rise for approximately 30 minutes. Bake until a rich brown for 25 to 30 minutes. Let cool for 20 minutes, then remove from pans.

Skillet Cornbread

Perfect for the wood-fired oven!

Ingredients:

1 1/2 cups (about 85/8 oz.) fine stone-ground
yellow cornmeal
1/4 cup all-purpose flour
2 teaspoons granulated sugar
1 teaspoon baking powder
1 teaspoon baking soda
1 teaspoon kosher salt
1 3/4 cups buttermilk
2 large eggs
3 tablespoons salted butter

Directions:

Heat oven to 450° F. Heat a 10" cast-iron skillet in the oven for 5 to 7 minutes.

Stir together the dry ingredients in a large bowl. Mix the buttermilk and eggs in a separate bowl. Add butter to skillet and return the skillet to the oven until the butter is melted. Combine the dry and wet ingredients just until combined. Pour the mixture into the skillet and place in the oven. Cook for 18– 20 minutes or until the bread is golden brown and pulls away from the sides of the skillet. Remove from skillet and cool slightly before serving.

Poppyseed Bread

By Margaret Lombardo

Ingredients:

3 eggs
1 ½ c lukewarm milk
1 pkg active dry yeast

1 1/8 c oil

2 ¼ c sugar

Mix all these ingredients together for 1 minute

Add

3 c flour (don't sift)

1 ½ tsp baking powder

1 ½ tsp salt

1 ½ tbsp. poppy seeds

1 ½ tsp almond butter (vanilla flavored)

Mix all these ingredients for 2 minutes

Place in greased bowl and move dough around to coat. Cover and let dough rise in a warm place until double. Punch down, then form into two loaves and place in greased bread pans. Let rise. Bake for one hour at 350 degrees. Let cool for 20 minutes.

Glaze:

¼ c orange juice

¾ c sugar

½ tsp each almond butter (vanilla flavored)

Beat 2 minutes. Slice bread and pour glaze over bread.

Desserts

Standard Pastry for One-Crust Pie

Mix together:

1 c sifted flour

½ tsp salt

Cut in with pastry blender:

½ c cold butter

Sprinkle with 2 tbsp water

Mix with fork until all the flour is moistened. Gather dough together and press firmly into a ball. Roll out on flour-covered board with rolling pin and place into a pie plate. Prick the bottom with a fork.

Double t

he recipe for a two-crust pie.

Fresh Berry Pie

Select ripe juicy berries. Berries picked at the height of the season are more flavorful require less sugar, and make the most delicious pies.

Wash berries, drain well. Then pick them over. Remove stems and hulls.

Line pie pan with your prepared

crust. Use the smaller or larger amount of sugar according to your taste and the sweetness of the fruit. Very tart fruit may require even more sugar.

For the filling:

Mix together:
1 to 1 ½ c sugar
1/3 c flour
½ tsp cinnamon
Mix lightly through,
4 c fresh berries

Pour berries into pastry-lined pie pan. Dot with 1 ½ tsp butter.

Cover with top crust which has slits cut in it. Bake until crust is nicely browned and juice begins to bubble through slits in crust. Serve slightly warm, not hot. Bake at 425 degrees for 35 to 45 minutes.

Supreme Apple Pie
Ingredients:

2 1/4 cups flour
1 tsp. salt
1 cup butter
5 to 7 Tbsp. ice cold water
6 cups thinly sliced or chopped peeled tart apples (half pears if desired)
3/4 cup sugar
1 Tbsp. cornstarch

1/2 tsp. ground cinnamon
1/4 tsp. ground nutmeg
1 Tbsp. lemon juice

Directions:

Heat oven to 400°

Crust: Mix flour and salt in large bowl. Cut in shortening using a pastry blender until mixture resembles course crumbs.

Add water, 1 Tbsp. at a time, mixing lightly with fork until flour mixture is evenly moistened and clings together when pressed into a ball. Divide dough in half; shape each half into 1/2 inch thick rounds. Wrap each dough round in plastic wrap; refrigerate for 15 minutes.

Toss apples with sugar, cornstarch, cinnamon, nutmeg and lemon juice in large bowl; set aside.

Place 1 dough round between two large sheets of plastic wrap; roll out dough with rolling pin to flatten slightly, working from center of dough to the edge. Turn over; continue rolling until dough round is about 2 inches larger that the diameter of an inverted 9''' pie plate.

Peel off the top piece of plastic wrap; invert dough into pie plate.

form bubbles that burst slowly. Cool. Serve with vanilla ice cream if desired.

The Best Pumpkin Pie

Use the same crust recipe as for the Supreme Apple Pie.

Ingredients:

1/2 Cup white sugar

1/4 Cup dark brown sugar

2 tsp. ground cinnamon

1/2 tsp. salt

1/2 tsp. ground ginger

1/4 tsp. ground nutmeg

1/4 tsp. ground cloves

2 Tbsp. canola oil

2 large eggs

1 tsp. vanilla

1 1/4 cups milk

1 15-oz. can pumpkin

Directions:

Preheat oven to 425° F

Make pie crust

In a large bowl stir together the white sugar, brown sugar, cinnamon, salt, ginger, cloves, and nutmeg; set aside. Mix together the pumpkin, oil, vanilla, eggs, and milk in a separate bowl until evenly blended. Add the pumpkin

Peel off remaining piece of plastic wrap; press dough evenly onto bottom and up side of pie plate, being careful not to stretch the dough.

Trim any dough hanging over the edge of the pie plate with sharp knife; reserve trimmings.

Fill pie plate with apple mixture; set aside. Roll out remaining dough, place over filling. Trim top crust about 1/2 inch beyond edge of pipe plate and fold edge of top crust under edge of bottom crust; pinch edges together to form a ridge. Flute edge by using two fingers to press a V shape into the crust edge.

Cut several slits near the center of the pie to allow steam to escape. Form leaves out of remaining dough if desired and place on top of crust.

Bake 45—50 min. or until juices

mixture to the dry ingredients and stir until fully blended. Pour into prepared crust and place on a cookie sheet in the oven.

Bake for 10 minutes, reduce temperature to 350° F and bake for 40-50 minutes or until a knife inserted in the center comes out clean. Cool on a metal rack. Top with whipped cream before serving.

Skillet Pineapple Upside Down Cake (Substitute apricots for pineapple if desired)

First prepare the pan:
Melt ½ c butter in heavy 10" skillet. Sprinkle ½ c brown sugar (packed) evenly over butter. Arrange drained pineapple (crushed may be used if drained properly) in attractive pattern on the butter-sugar coating. Decorate with pecan halves and cherries if desired. Preheat oven to 350 degrees.

Sift together:

1 ½ c sifted flour

1 c sugar

2 tsp baking powder

½ tsp salt

Add,

1/3 c soft shortening or butter
2/3 c milk

1 tsp vanilla extract

½ tsp lemon flavoring, if desired

Beat for 2 minutes.

Add, 1 egg and continue to beat for 2 more minutes.

Pour cake batter over fruit. Bake for 40 to 50 minutes until toothpick stuck into center of cake comes out clean. Immediately turn upside down on serving plate. Leave pan over cake a few minutes. Brown sugar mixture will run down over cake. Serve warm with whipped cream.

Coffee Cake

Mix thoroughly:
¾ c sugar
¼ c soft shortening or butter
1 egg
Stir in:
½ c milk
Sift together, and stir in:
1 ½ c sifted flour
2 tsp baking powder
½ tsp salt
½ tsp cinnamon

Directions:

Spread batter in greased and floured 9" square pan or 10" skillet. Sprinkle with ½ brown sugar packed and 1 ½ tsp cinnamon.

Bake until toothpick stuck into center of cake comes out clean. Serve warm, fresh from the oven with butter on the side. Bake on 375° for 25 to 35 minutes. Makes nine 3" squares.

Apple Brown Betty
Use a cast-iron skillet or baking pan

Ingredients:

Four granny smith or red apples, peeled, cored, and sliced

For topping:
1/4 cup brown sugar
1/4 cup oats
2 T flour
2 T melted butter
1 t cinnamon

For cake:
Use your favorite yellow cake mix or pineapple upside-down cake recipe on previous page.

Directions:
Heat oven to 350°

Mix topping ingredients together and place on the bottom of a greased pan. Layer sliced apples next, then pour cake batter on top and bake until a toothpick inserted in the center comes out clean. Let cool for 15 minutes then, flip over onto a plate.

Baked Half Apples
by Maria McKenzie
These are well-suited for the wood-fired oven. Half an apple is just the right serving for children.

Ingredients:
4-5 Large Red Apples (8-10 halves)
Brown Sugar (about ½ to ¾ cup)
Real Butter (about 6-8 teaspoons)
1.5 to 2 cups Apple Cider
Several Ceylon cinnamon sticks

Instructions:
Cut the ends off of the apples and core the centers.

Slice the apples into halves and place face-down in a baking dish.

Sprinkle brown sugar over the apples and pour in the apple cider.

Randomly place dots of butter between some of the apples.

Place cinnamon sticks throughout the dish, making sure they're down into the cider.

Cover the baking dish with aluminum foil and bake slowly at 350° F until apples are soft enough to cut with a fork (about 45 minutes).

Serve warm.

Whole Baked Apples With Raisons

Ingredients:
4 apples
1/2 C brown sugar
4 pats butter
1 t cinnamon
1/2 t ground nutmeg
1/2 cup raisons

Directions:
Slice the tops off of the apples and core out the centers to remove seeds, but do not go all the way through to the bottom. Place apples in a baking dish with 1/2 cup water. Mix remaining ingredients and stuff the apple centers. Replace the tops if desired. Bake at 350° F until apples are soft enough to cut with a fork (about 45 minutes).

Note: We put these in the oven after the main and side dishes have been served and they cook just in time for dessert.

5-Cup Dessert Salad
No cooking needed!

Mix together in a large bowl:
1 cup drained chunk pineapple
1 cup sour cream
1 cup drained mandarin oranges
1 cup coconut
1 cup mini plain or multi-colored marshmallows

Cover with plastic wrap and chill for five hours or more. *Hint: use full cans of fruit and add more marshmallows if desired.*

Decadent Adult S'Mores

Ingredients:
8 oz of your favorite chocolate
1 jigger brandy (if desired)
Graham crackers
Marshmallows

Directions:
Get the oven, smoker or grill ready and on low heat. Place chocolate and brandy in a small casserole dish and top with the marshmallows. Cook until the marshmallows are browned. Serve with graham crackers. Vary the amount by the number of people being served.

Recipes for the Smoker and Grill

Smoked Turkey

Prep Time: 30 mins
Cook Time: 12 hrs.

Ingredients:
2 -3 tablespoons extra virgin olive oil
14 -16 pound turkey, fresh or thawed completely
2 -3 tablespoons lemon and herb seasoning
2 tsp mixed garlic granules
2 tsp course salt
2 tsp freshly ground black pepper
5 -6 wood chunks: hickory, apple, cherry, oak, pecan or other smoking hardwood soaked in water at least overnight (not chips)
10 -15 lbs good quality charcoal (Do not use self-lighting charcoal or charcoal lighter fluid)

Directions:
(Wash thawed turkey thoroughly, inside and out. Pat dry with a paper towel.

Coat turkey with olive oil. Season inside and out with lemon-herb seasoning, granulated garlic, and salt and pepper to taste. Refrigerate until

ready to start smoking.

Soak 5-6 fairly large chunks of hardwood in water for as long as possible. DO NOT USE CHIPS!

Prep the smoker:
12 hours before mealtime, prepare the outdoor water smoker as follows:

Place 10 pounds charcoal in the fire-pan and conservatively light the charcoal- just enough to keep it burning with a very low flame.

(Use an electric starter, or a butane torch, or place charcoal under your oven broiler just until lit. DO NOT use liquid charcoal lighter unless you want kerosene flavored turkey!) Place 2-3 chunks of wet hardwood on top of the charcoal, place water-pan above fire-pan, and fill with water.

Place turkey on the rack above the water-pan and cover the smoker.

After about 6 hours, check the smoker. Stir up the charcoal and add a little more if necessary.

Place remaining soaked hardwood chunks on top of charcoal, add more water if necessary, close the smoker for another 5-6 hours.

It is almost impossible to overcook the turkey using this method, because it is cooking at a very low temperature.

If the weather is freezing or below, add about 2-3 hours to the cooking time unless you are using a brick smoker which retains more heat.

The turkey is done when the leg can be moved easily

or when meat thermometer reading is 180°.

Smoked Barbeque Chicken

Ingredients:
1 or two whole chickens
Olive oil
Apple or Cherry wood soaked in water for at least two hours
1 bottle of barbeque sauce
1 or two bags of dry barbeque seasoning

Directions:
Heat smoker to 200-150 degrees F. Start it 45 min before smoking the chicken.

Mix dry seasoning with enough olive oil to make paste and pat all over the chicken. Place the wood on the hot coals and put the chicken in the smoker. When the chicken is almost done, baste it in barbecue sauce. Cook until the internal temperature is 165 degrees, then remove it from the smoker. Cover with foil or place in a roasting pan with a lid for 15-20 minutes to finish cooking and set up for carving. Serve with additional barbecue sauce and your favorite side dishes.

Note: This chicken can also be smoked in a wood-fired oven. Place wood chips in the oven under chicken placed on a rack.

Grilled Mediterranean Beef or Turkey Burgers
4 servings

Ingredients:

1 lb ground beef or turkey

1 cup crumbled feta cheese

1/2 cup kalamata olive, chopped (I usually use chopped salad olives)

1 teaspoon dried oregano

1 teaspoon Italian seasoning

1 teaspoon dried parsley

1 teaspoon dried basil (optional)

1 teaspoon onion powder

1/2 teaspoon garlic powder

ground black pepper, to taste

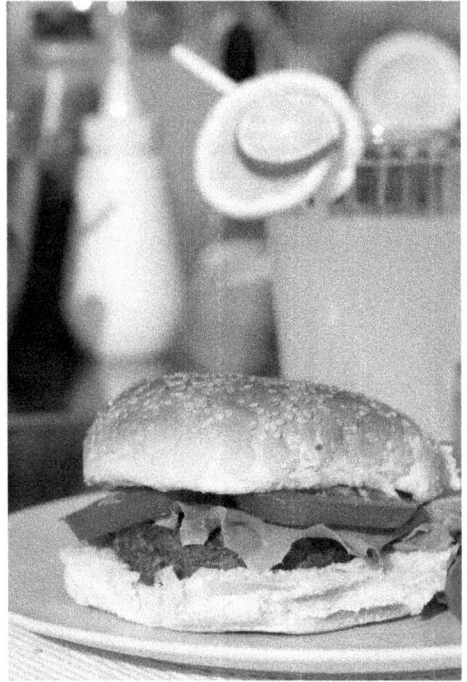

Directions:

Combine all the ingredients in a large bowl.

Form into 4 patties, then grill.

Serve on regular burger buns with tomatoes and mayo, or on pita with tahini, tomatoes and lettuce.

The Perfect Grilled Hamburger

Ingredients:

Ground beef or turkey

1 medium egg per lb. of meat

Garlic salt to taste

Pepper to taste

1 Tablespoon Worcester Sauce per Lb.

1-2 Tablespoons Heinz 57 per Lb.

1/2 cup bread crumbs per lb.

Chopped onions

Directions:

Beat egg(s) in a large bowl, then add all other ingredients and mix well.

Shape into patties and place on the grill. While cooking, do not press down on the burger or it will dry out. When brown, flip over to brown the other side. Do not overcook and keep off of direct flame to avoid charring. .

Serve with buns, lettuce, and sliced tomato. If desired, leave the onions out of the mix and grill some sliced onions to serve on the side. These burgers have so much flavor that people likely won't need to add condiments. For those who are gluten-free, serve with salad or gluten-free buns.

Roasted Vegetables
For the Oven or Grill

This is one of our favorites because is easy, fast, and delicious and can be served with almost any main dish.

Ingredients:
1 T fresh or dried rosemary
1 T fresh or dried thyme
1 t course sea salt
1 t pepper
1 clove garlic, chopped
3 T extra virgin olive oil
2 T butter

1 medium green pepper chopped in 1" pieces
1 medium yellow pepper chopped
1 medium onion chopped
1 medium yellow or green zucchini cut into 1/2" slices
Or use other veggies of your choice such as mushrooms, asparagus, or scallions.

Directions:
For the grill: make a pan out of heavy duty aluminum foil with 1/2" edges and place on a hot grill. For the oven: Place a metal or ceramic pan in the oven.

Place olive oil and butter in the pan together and add garlic. After the butter is melted, add the salt, pepper, rosemary and thyme and mix thoroughly. Add the cut vegetables and stir to coat. If desired, add chopped tomato the last cou-

ple of minutes of cooking. Cook for 15-20 minutes or until desired doneness and serve.

Grilled Onion Flower

Ingredients:
Large onion (any variety)
Butter
Salt
Pepper
Diced Garlic

Directions:

1. Melt butter in a small pot with salt, pepper, and diced garlic (substitute garlic powder if necessary).

2. Cut then top end off of the onion, place the onion on a cutting block with the root end on the bottom, Cut through the onion from the top almost to the bottom in slices approximately 1/3" thick. After cutting, place the onion on a piece of aluminum foil large enough to cover the entire onion.

3. Open up the cut onion and pour the butter mixture into the onion flower.

4. Wrap the onion in the aluminum foil, and twist the top of the foil together.

Place on the grill and cook for 20-30 minutes or until desired doneness is achieved.

Roasted Corn on the Grill

Pull back the husks of ears of corn and pull out the silky strings, then pour melted butter over the corn, and sprinkle salt and pepper on as desired. replace the husks. Put the corn on the brill with husks on to keep it moist inside.

Cook corn for about 30 minutes and it will be perfectly cooked! Note that the husk will burn but your corn will be roasted to perfection.

Cedar Planked Salmon

Ingredients:
Salmon
Olive oil
Salt
Lemon pepper
Fresh cut lemon quarters

Directions:
Prepare the plank
Season the salmon

Green Lentil Soup

Cook on the grill or in a wood-fired oven until done (145°F)
Serve with lemon wedges

Shrimp on the Barbie

Cook these last because they take only a short time!

Ingredients:

Jumbo shrimp or prawns
Olive oil or butter
Thyme
Salt
Pepper
Other herbs as desired

Directions:

Place shrimp on skewers so they lie flat on the grill.

Melt butter or use olive oil, mix in seasonings.

Baste shrimp with mixture.

Cook for 2 minutes on one side, then turn over and cook for 2 more minutes or until shrimp turns pink.

Lobster on the Grill

Save for last because they cook fast.

Ingredients:

As many lobster tails as you wish to cook
Melted butter

How to Use a Cedar Plank on the Grill

A unique and delicious way to grill food is by using a wooden plank. This is a surefire way to get delicious results and wow your dinner guests. The smoke created from the plank sitting directly above a lit burner infuses the meat with unsurpassed grilled flavor.

Using a plank is simple:

1.   Soak the plank in water for at least an hour and pat it dry

2.   Pre-heat your grill on HIGH for 10 minutes

3.   Coat both sides of the plank with olive oil then place the seasoned meat on it

4.   Place the plank on the grill directly over the lit burner or coals and reduce the heat to MEDIUM-LOW

5.   Cook the meat to its desired doneness

6.   Cedar planks are ideal for salmon but don't be afraid to try other meats with it. Pork cooks well on a maple plank and lamb is delicious on alder.

7.   Note: Make sure to be careful while handling the plank after grilling and that it is fully extinguished before discarding.

Salt

Garlic powder or diced garlic cloves

Directions:

Wash lobster tails

Melt butter and stir in seasonings. With lobster tails bottom side up, pour seasoned butter on them, and place on the grill for three minutes. Turn tails over and cook until done.

Slice tails in half, lengthwise, and service with more butter drizzled on top.

Baked Potatoes on the Grill

Ingredients:

Large baking potatoes of your choice

Melted butter

Salt

Pepper

Garlic powder (if desired)

Directions:

Start these first because they take at least 40 minutes to cook. Prick each potato all around with a fork so steam can vent. Wrap each potato in aluminum foil separately. Place on the grill but not too close to the fire so they won't burn. It is best to cook them at a lower temperature. When a knife

inserts easily they are done. Remove from the grill. Open each potato and cut in half, then drizzle with melted butter and sprinkle with salt, pepper, and garlic powder.

Grilled Pork Chops

Serves 6

Ingredients:

1/2 cup water

1/3 cup light soy sauce

1/4 cup vegetable oil

3 tablespoons lemon pepper seasoning

2 garlic cloves, minced

6 pork loin chops, fat removed

Directions:

In deep bowl- mix all marinade ingredients.

Marinate chops at least 2 hours.

Remove from marinade and cook over medium-high heat on greased grill for no more than 15 minutes or until done. Cooking time for second side is shorter by 1-2 minutes. 3/4" or thinner, 5-6 minutes maximum per side, thicker than 3/4" 6-7 minutes maximum per side. DO NOT OVER-GRILL, chops will become tough. After 2 minutes grilling on a side, rotate chops 45 degrees for even cooking. Turn over when juices pool on upper surface and meat appears to be cooked half-way through.

Grilled Trout or Snapper

Ingredients:
Small fish, about 1 1/2 lbs each
Dried or fresh sage
Dried or fresh mint
Lemon slices
Salt and pepper

Directions:
Cut fish lengthwise along the side, and open it up. Brush both sides with olive oil. Mix herbs, salt, and pepper and place inside the fish along with lemon slices. Close the fish and place on the grill or in the oven.

To Add Smoke Flavor

Soak wood chips in water for 20 minutes. Cut a 10-12" piece of foil, place the wood chips in the center and fold the foil over the top. Cut three holes in the top with a knife. Place on the coals or on the burner, or inside the oven. As the chips heat they will release smoke.

Tip for Grilling

Place items that take longer to cook such as potatoes and carrots on the grill first, then add other items so that they all finish cooking at the same time.

Smoking Meat

Meat can be smoked in a smoker or on a barbecue grill. The key to success is to cook at very low temperatures over live coals.

The benefit is a tender, juicy and flavorful meat that is worth the time to cook in this manner.

Keep the fire burning and don't let it go out. The key is to use indirect heat, and not allow the meat to get near the coals.

To use a grill as a smoker: push lit coals on either side of the grill, leaving a space in the center for a foil pan with hot water. The water creates a moist environment which is critical for smoking, and it also stabilizes temperatures. Add herbs to the water to flavor the food.

Place the grill on top of this set up and put the meat on this. Close the lid. Cook at 225 to 250 degrees F.

A meat thermometer probe placed inside the top vent of the grill lid and hanging down inside the grill will work well.

Regulate air by using the grill vents.

Consistent temperature is the key to a good finished product.

Add more coals as needed to keep the fire going.

Ribs, pulled pork, and brisken will take several hours to cook.

Don't lift the lid to check the meat. Every time the lid is opened it adds 15 minutes of cooking time. Open only when you need to add more coals to keep the temperature steady.

Use wood chips soaked for 20 to 30 minutes in water and place in the smoker box or on the coals to add flavor. Hickory is good for all meats. Mesquite is used for beef and poultry. Use Alder for fish and seafood. Apple and Cherry add great flavor to poultry and pork. Maple is mild and sweet and is best used with poultry, pork, or cheese

Smoking Time Chart

Food	Size	Smoking time	Temp
Turkey Leg	2 lbs	3-4 hours	225
Whole Turkey	12-16 lbs	35 min per lb.	225
Whole Turkey - fast cook	12-16 lbs	18 min per lb.	275
Whole chicken	3-5 lbs	4-5 hours	225
Chicken quarters	Med	3-3 1/2 hours	225
Brisket	6-12 lbs	45 min - 1 hr per lb	225
Meatloaf	2 lbs	2 hours	250
Hamburger	3/4" thick	1 1/2 - 2 hours	275
Prime Rib	4-8 lbs	45 min per lb	225
Baby Back Ribs	Full slab	4-5 hours	225
Pork Butt Sliced	4-6 lbs	1 - 1 1/4 lbs per lb	225
Pork Butt Pulled	6- 8 lbs	1 hr per lb	225
Pre-cooked Whole Ham	6-8 lbs	35 min per lb	225
Venison Roast	4-6 lbs	45 -60 min per lb	225
Jerky	1/4" strips	12-16 hrs.	140
Corn on the Cob	6-12	1 1/2 hours	225
Potatoes	Medium	1 1 1/2 hours	225
Jalapeno Poppers	Large	2 hours	225
Mac-N-Cheese	1 1/2 lbs	1 hour	225
Chocolate (for s'mores)	8 oz	30 - 60 minutes	225

Recipes for the Kettle over an open fire, pot on the grill, or in an oven

By Marge Padgitt

This is a favorite at my house during fall and winter months

Ingredients:

2 Tbsp. olive oil

6 medium carrots, diced

1 large yellow onion, diced

4 bay leaves

1 Tbsp. minced garlic

2 1/2 quarts chicken broth

1 bag green lentils (1 ½ lb. bag)

1/2 t. ground black pepper

1 tsp. sea salt

1 lb. diced ham (optional)

Directions:

In a large Dutch oven or pot, heat olive oil over medium heat. Add onion, carrot, and garlic. Cook for 10 minutes, stirring frequently, or until onion is translucent. If desired, add ham and cook for 5 minutes or until lightly browned. Add chicken broth, lentils, bay leaves, pepper and salt. Bring to a boil, reduce heat and simmer, covered, for 25 to 30 minutes in the oven or until lentils are tender. Remove and discard bay leaves. Serve immediately.

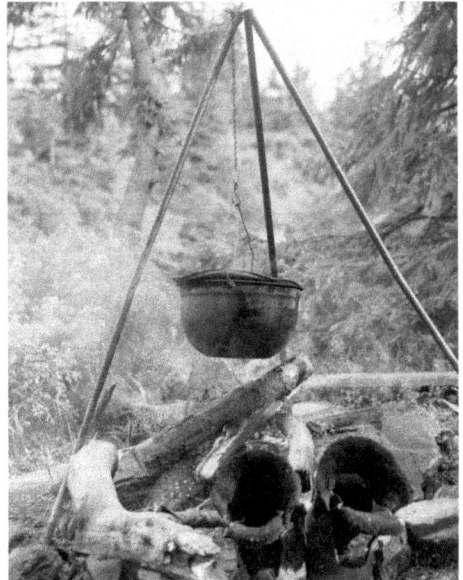

Minestrone Soup

This is one of my Italian grandmother's recipes that has been a family favorite for years.

Ingredients

2 T extra-virgin olive oil

1 large onion, diced

2 T chopped fresh basil

3 - 4 cloves garlic, minced

2 stalks celery, diced

1 large carrot, cut in slices

1/3 pound green beans, trimmed and cut into 1/2-inch pieces (about 1 1/2 cups)

1 t dried oregano

1 t dried basil

Sea salt and freshly ground pepper
1 28 -ounce can diced tomatoes
(or cut up fresh)
1 14 -ounce can crushed tomatoes
6 cups low-sodium chicken broth
1 15 -ounce can kidney beans or
white Northern beans, drained
and rinsed
1 cup elbow or small shell pasta
1/3 cup finely grated parmesan
cheese

Directions

Heat the olive oil in a large pot
over medium-high heat. Add the
onion and cook until translucent,
about 4 minutes. Add the garlic
and cook 30 seconds. Add the
celery and carrot and cook until
they begin to soften, about 5
minutes. Stir in the green beans,
dried oregano and basil, 3/4 teaspoon salt, and pepper to taste;
cook 3 more minutes.
Add the diced and crushed tomatoes and the chicken broth to the
pot and bring to a boil. Reduce
the heat to medium low and simmer 10 minutes. Stir in the kidney
beans and pasta and cook until
the pasta and vegetables are tender, about 10 minutes. Season
with salt. Ladle into bowls and
top with the parmesan and
chopped basil.

Yummy Vegetable Soup

Ingredients:

One 32 ounce box of vegetable
broth
1 T olive oil
One large onion, chopped
Three large carrots, sliced thin
1 T minced garlic
Three stalks celery, chopped
1 green or yellow zucchini,
chopped
Salt and pepper to taste
1 t thyme leaves
2 Bay leaves

Directions

Heat the olive oil in a large pot
over medium-high heat. Add the
onion and cook until translucent,
about 4 minutes. Add the garlic
and cook 30 seconds. Add the celery and carrot and cook until they
begin to soften, about 5 minutes.
Stir in the vegetable broth, seasonings, and zucchini. Simmer for
about 20 minutes or until the vegetables are tender. Remove bay
leaves before serving.

Beef Soup:

Follow directions above using beef
broth instead of vegetable broth.
Add chunks of beef.

Sausage and Vegetable Soup

Follow directions above and add

Split Pea Soup

Ingredients:

2 T olive oil

1 package dried split peas

One large onion, diced

2 cloves garlic, diced

Three large diced carrots

2 Stalks celery, diced

Salt

Pepper

2-3 Bay leaves

32 oz Chicken or vegetable broth

Water

4 cubes chicken bullion

Directions:

Sauté onions and garlic in pot for 3 minutes. Add carrots and celery and cook for 5 minutes. Add all other ingredients and cook for 40 - 50 minutes.

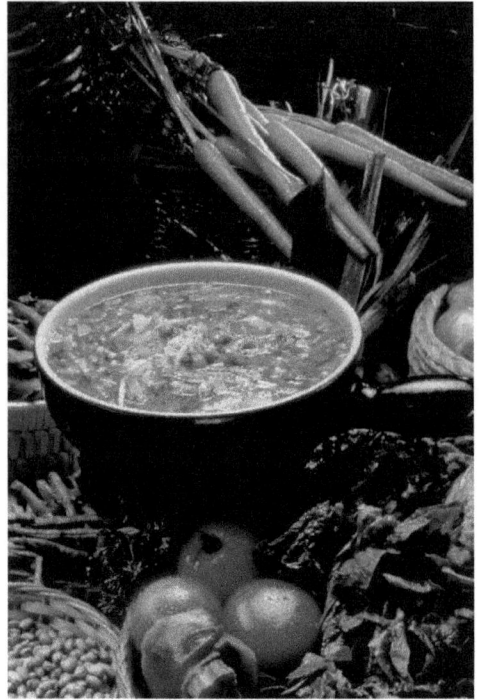

Chicken Chili

Ingredients:

1 T olive oil

1 lb boneless skinless chicken breasts, cut into 1-in. cubes

1 C chopped onion

1 C chopped bell pepper

1 T paprika

1 1/2 t oregano

2 minced garlic cloves

1 can black beans, drained

1 can Great Northern beans, drained and rinsed

1 14 oz can diced tomatoes, undrained

1 C chicken stock

1 C frozen corn (if desired)

Instructions:

Heat oil in large skillet or Dutch oven over medium heat. Add chicken, pepper, garlic, and onion and cook for 6- 8 minutes until chicken is lightly browned. Add remaining ingredients, stir and cook for 20 - 30 minutes.

Tandoor Oven Recipes

Naan Flatbread

Ingredients:

1 envelope active dry yeast

5 T sugar

1C warm water (110°)

1 egg, beaten

3 T milk

2 t salt

4 ½- 5 cups all-purpose flour

1 T vegetable oil

4 T unsalted, melted butter

Directions:

1. Place yeast and 1 T sugar in 1/4 c water and let stand until foamy, about 5-10 minutes. Stir in the remaining sugar and water, the egg, milk, and salt. Add 4 cups of the flour and stir or place in a mixer with a dough hook. Add more flour if necessary. This should take 6 to 8 minutes.

2. Use 1/2 T of the oil to lightly oil a large bowl. Place dough in the bowl, brush the top with the remaining oil, cover with a clean towel. Let rise in a warm location until doubled in size (1 - 1 ½ hours). Meanwhile, get your tandoor or bake oven heated. Punch down the dough and pinch off 2-inch pieces. Roll into 14-16 balls. Place the balls on a lightly floured baking sheet and cover with a lightly dampened clean kitchen towel. Let rise for 30 minutes.

3. Roll out a dough ball on a lightly floured cutting board to form a disk about 5 inches in diameter. Slap the dough back and forth from one hand to the other to stretch int into an elongated 7 -8 inch circle. Stretch dough in to a teardrop shape, then throw it onto the inside wall of the tandoor oven, or place on the floor of your bake oven. Cook until the bottom is browned and toe top is puffed, about 2 - 4 minutes. Brush with butter. Invert and cook in the same manner for 2-4 minutes. Brush with butter, and serve whole or cut into wedges.

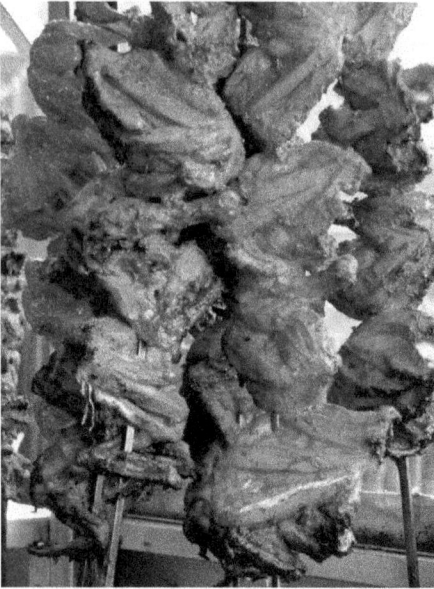

Tandoori Chicken Photo: Fotolia

Tandoori Chicken

Ingredients:

6 Tablespoons lime juice
1/3 C plain yogurt
1 1/2 t salt
1 t ground turmeric
1 t ground coriander
1 t ground cumin
1/2 t ground ginger
1/2 t garlic powder
1/2 t cayenne pepper
1/4 t ground cinnamon
2 t ground cloves
2 T vegetable or olive oil
3 lbs. skinless chicken thighs
If desired for extra kick: 1-2 jalapeno chilies, seeded and minced

Directions:

Heat the tandoor oven (or bake oven) to 425° or higher. Stir together all ingredients and 1 tablespoon of the oil. Cut chicken in large chunks, and rub the spice mixture all over the chicken. Place in a large plastic freezer bag and let sit in the refrigerator for 8 hours or overnight.

Heat the tandoor oven (or bake oven) to 425° or higher. Place chicken on metal kabobs and place in the oven. Bake until the internal temperature is 165°.

Tandoori Vegetables

Ingredients:

2 large yellow onions
1 green pepper
1 red pepper
1 box button mushrooms
2 T olive oil
2 T melted butter
1/2 t garlic powder
1/2 t sea salt
1/2 t black pepper
1/2 t turmeric
1/2 t ground cumin

Directions:

Heat the tandoor or bake oven to at least 400°

Mix olive oil, butter, and spices in a

small bowl. Keep warm on the stove or in the oven.

Cut onions and peppers into large pieces. Place onions, peppers, and whole button mushrooms on metal skewers. Brush seasoned oil onto the vegetables, then place into the tandoor oven. Cook for 15-20 minutes, depending on desired doneness. Remove vegetables from the skewer with a large fork, and serve on a platter.

Tandoori Shrimp. Photo: Fotolia-maryskin

Tandoori Shrimp

Ingredients:

1 lb. uncooked large shrimp or prawns, shelled and deveined, tails left on.
Olive oil
1/2 Tbsp chipped cilantro
1 lemon or lime, cut into wedges

Marinade ingredients:

1/3 cup Greek yogurt
1/2 tsp Garam Masala (blend of Indian spices available online)
1 tsp finely minced garlic
1/4 tsp chili powder
2 Tbsp lime juice
1 Tbsp oil
1/2 tsp sea salt
1/3 tsp turmeric or curry powder

Directions:

In a small bowl stir together all of the marinade ingredients, add the shrimp and let rest for 30 minutes to two hours. Skewer shrimp on stainless steel or soaked bamboo skewers.

Baste shrimp with olive oil and place shrimp inside the Tandoor. The shrimp will cook at a different rate depending on how hot the oven is so watch carefully. When done, remove from the oven and place on a plate. Garnish with chipped cilantro or parsley and serve with lemon or lime wedges. Serve with rice.

Appetizers

Cheese Board

Great as an appetizer before dinner or with cocktails.

Ingredients:
Variety of Cheeses: Smoked cheddar, Swiss, Brie, Farmer, Gouda, Port wine, etc.
Small artisan bread slices such as baguette
Deluxe crackers
Red and green grapes
Nuts, olives, and a variety of chutneys, mustard, jams

Directions:
Take cheese out of the refrigerator one hour before serving. Place cheese and other items on a platter, Place a cheese board and knives out for guests to use.

Fresh Salsa and Chips Appetizer

Geno and I had fresh salsa during a trip to Cancun, Mexico and it tasted so good we tried to replicate it when we got
home. We do can salsa every year using tomatoes and peppers from Geno's garden, but we much prefer fresh.

Ingredients:
Two large fresh tomatoes, chopped
One small—medium yellow onion, diced
One small green pepper, diced
Several springs fresh cilantro, chopped
Sea salt and pepper to taste

Directions:
Combine all ingredients in a bowl, garnish with a sprig of cilantro, and enjoy with tortilla chips.

Antipasto

Ingredients:
One or two containers Mozzarella cheese balls in oil (refrigerated section)
One container cherry tomatoes
One can whole black olives
One jar stuffed green olives (if desired)
Italian dressing to taste

Mix together and refrigerate until time to serve. Place fancy toothpicks next to the plate.

Bruschetta

You'll need the oven or grill for this one. This is always a favorite at our house.

Ingredients:

1 can diced tomatoes, or chop two large tomatoes.
1 t fresh or dried oregano
2 t fresh or dried basil
Salt and pepper to taste
1 loaf French bread
1/4 C chopped black olives
1 T cider vinegar

Instructions:

Mix all ingredients except bread. Brush oil on bread slices and bake for 6 to 8 minutes until crisp and light brown. Turn once. Cool on rack. Spoon tomato mixture on bread slices and serve.

With cheese: If desired, sprinkle parmesan cheese on top or spoon 1 teaspoon goat cheese on the bread prior to the tomato mixture.

Stuffed Mushrooms

Ingredients:

12 large fresh mushrooms, stems removed and chopped
1 8 oz package cream cheese, softened
1/2 lb imitation crab meat, flaked
2 C butter
2 cloves minced garlic
Salt and pepper to taste
8 oz. dry chicken flavored stuffing mix

Instructions:

Heat oven or grill to 350 degrees. Melt butter in a medium saucepan, add garlic and cook for 5 minutes over medium heat.

Mix mushroom stems and remaining ingredients in a bowl. If desired, add red pepper flakes. Stuff the mushrooms with the mixture.

Bake on a baking sheet for 10 - 12 minutes or until browned.

Note: You can stuff mushrooms with just about anything and they'll taste great!

Hot and Cold Drinks

Hibiscus Tea

Here's something you can do with edible hibiscus flowers besides look at them:

Ingredients:

6 cups water
2 cups dried hibiscus flowers
3/4 cup granulated sugar (or to taste)

Directions:

Bring six cups of water to a boil, add the flowers and sugar. Stir while bringing to a boil, then boil for one minute. Turn off the heat and pour into a class container and let cool and steep for two hours.

Stain through a sieve, pressing down to extract the liquid. Taste, and if too sweet add more water, if too tart add more sugar. Keep in refrigerator until ready to serve over ice.

Perfect Sweet Tea

Ingredients:

Your favorite tea (in bags or loose tea in a tea ball)
1 cup sugar or honey

7 cups water

Directions:

Make a simple syrup by mixing the 1 c sugar or honey with 1 c water in a small saucepan and boil while stirring until the sugar is dissolved. Turn off the heat and let cool. Make tea to desired strength in 6 cups water. Pour syrup into tea and adjust taste with extra water or tea as needed. Keep frigerated.

Hot Apple Cider

For cool fall nights

Ingredients:

2 quarts apple cider
1/2 cup brown sugar
1 tsp whole allspice
1 tsp whole cloves
1/4 tsp salt
1/8 tsp nutmeg
3 or 4 cinnamon sticks

Directions:

Place the cider and spices in pot on the grill and heat to boiling. Move to side and simmer for 20 minutes. Strain and serve.

Mojitos

Ingredients:

Fresh mint from your garden
Vodka
Simple syrup
Lime juice
Sprite or club soda

Directions:

Crush a few mint leaves in the bottom of a tall glass. Add ice. Add 1 jigger of vodka, a splash of simple syrup, 1 T lime juice, and Sprite or Club Soda and stir.

Sangria Punch

Ingredients:

1 each sliced lemon and orange
3 T brown sugar
1 bottle sangria or dry red wine
3/4 C pineapple juice
3/4 cup orange juice
1 can sprite or 7-up
1 cup ice cubes
1 1/2 oz vodka
1 can orange soda

Directions:

Mix ingredients and serve. It won't last long.

Cucumber Sangria

Ingredients:

1 seedless cucumber, thinly sliced
1 lime, thinly sliced
12 fresh mint leaves
1 small honeydew melon
1/4 c lime juice
1/4 c honey or sugar
1 750 ml bottle semi-dry white wine
1 liter bottle carbonated water

Directions:

Cut the melon in half, remove the seeds and cut off the rind. Cut the melon into thin slices. In a large pitcher or punch bowl combine wine, melon, cucumber lime slices and mint leaves. Stir together lime juice and honey or sugar in a separate bowl, then mix with melon mixture. Cover and chill for at least two hours. To serve, stir in carbonated water then pour into glasses. Garnish with mint.

Perfect Lemonade

Ingredients

2 c sugar

2 c lemon juice or freshly squeezed lemons to make 2 cups juice

8 cups water

Directions:

Mix 1 cup water and the sugar in a small saucepan to make a simple syrup. Bring to a boil and stir to dissolve the sugar. Turn off the heat and let cool, them place in the refrigerator until ready to serve. Add lemon juice and remaining water to the simple syrup and serve. For pink lemonade, add a few drops of Grenadine. For limeade, substitute limes for the lemon.

Party Punch

Ingredients:

1/2 gallon lime or raspberry sherbet

1 2-liter bottle 7-up or Sprite

1 can frozen grape juice

1 can frozen fruit juice

Directions:

Just before the party starts put liquids into a punch bowl and mix thoroughly. Drop small ice-cream scoopfuls or serving spoon size scoops of sherbet into the bowl. The frozen items make the use of ice unnecessary.

Mojitos

Ingredients:

6 limes

12 Fresh mint sprigs

1/2 c Simple syrup

6 jiggers white rum

20 oz sparkling water

Directions:

Muddle mint in the bottom of tall glasses. Mix the rest of the ingredients in a pitcher and serve over ice. Adjust recipe to taste.

Mimosas

Mix 1/2 glass sparkling wine and 1/2 glass orange juice. Yum!

Shirley Temple

A non-alcoholic drink for everyone.

Ingredients:

Lemon-lime soda

Grenadine

Maraschino Cherries

Pour soda over ice. Pour in a dash of grenadine and stir. Top with a

Maraschino cherry.

Frozen Cosmopolitan

Ingredients:
10 oz citrus-flavored vodka
1/2 c lime juice
2 c cranberry juice
2 c water
4 ice cube trays

Directions:
Mix liquids in a pitcher. Divide between the ice cube trays and freeze 4 hours or overnight. Just before serving, empty cubes into a large bowl and crush with a potato masher or place into a blender and pulse. Spoon into martini glasses and serve immediately.

Margaritas

Ingredients:
3/4 c tequila
1/2 c fresh lime juice
1/2 c Triple Sec or Cointreau
1/2 c water
1 sliced lime
Kosher salt

Directions:
In a pitcher combine tequila, lime juice, Triple Sec and 1/2 c water. Rub the rims of four glasses with a lime slice and dip into salt to coat.

Add ice to the glasses. Pour liquid into the glasses and garnish with a lime slice.

Quick Orange Punch

Ingredients:
1/2 gallon orange sherbet
1 6 oz. can frozen orange juice concentrate
1 2-liter bottle ginger ale

Place frozen orange juice and sherbet in a punch bowl. Allow to thaw for 15 minutes. Add ginger ale and stir. Serve immediately.

Halloween Punch

Ingredients:
1 .13 oz envelope unsweetened orange soft drink mix
1 .13 oz envelope unsweetened grape soft drink mix
2 c sugar
3 quarts cold water
1 liter ginger ale

Pour water into a disposable plastic glove, seal the end with a rubber band and freeze. Mix ingredients, then remove ice hand from glove, and place in the punch for a spooky effect.

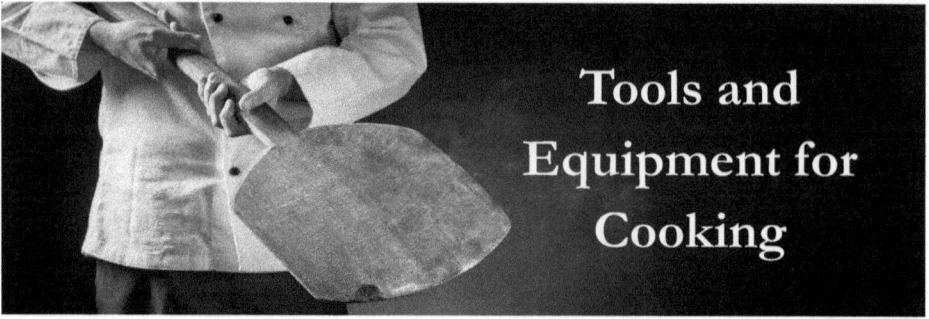

Tools and Equipment for Cooking

There are a few must-have pieces of equipment that any outdoor chef needs, whether for the oven, grill, smoker, or campfire:

1. **A good pizza peel** or two. Some people like wood peels, others prefer stainless steel. We use both. We use a wood peel to make the pizza on and transfer it to the oven, then use a thin stainless steel peel to remove pizza from the oven. When cooking casseroles, the steel peel comes in very handy as well. We use long-handled peels to reach the back part of the oven without getting burned. Find peels at fornobravo.com.

2. **Rocking Pizza Cutter:** Forget the small rolling cutters. Get a good stainless steel rocking pizza cutter and make your life easier. Camp Chef Italia makes a good cutter.

3. **An oven brush:** Get a long-handled brush to remove ashes. Napoleon makes a BBQ Dragon Brush 'n Rake.

4. **Oven mop:** We use a rag mop dipped in water and rung out, then wipe the bottom of the oven to clean it. No need to scrub heavily - just a quick swipe will do. This works better while the oven is warm. Don't use soap. A few ashes on pizza dough won't matter.

5. **Grilling tools:** long-handled spatula, tongs, knife, and fork are must -haves. If you like seafood, get some skewers, too. We found some nice sets by Weber.

6. **Grill brush:** May styles and sizes are available. Clean your grill after it cools down but is still warm. Napoleon makes a nice triple-row grill brush.

7. **Basting brush:** Cuisinart makes a stainless steel sauce pot and

basting brush. Keep it warm on the grill.

8. **Fish basket for the grill:** These measure about 5" x 26" and can handle a fish, or shrimp. This makes turning easier and the fish won't stick to the grill. Can also be used for vegetables.

9. **Skewers:** These can be used for shrimp or veggies. We prefer stainless steel instead of wood skewers because they last forever.

10. **Long-handled** wooden spoon and ladle for soups and stews.

11. **Cast iron camping tripod:** to hold your stewpot easily. Available at Amazon.com

12. **Cast iron stew pot:** Place right on the fire or hang from a tripod. Carolina Cooker makes a 5 gallon pot for big crowds. Cabela's caries a 10", 12", 14" and 16" diameter Dutch Ovens.

13. **Dutch oven lid lifter:** Lodge carries a nice lid lifter. You'll want this when cooking over an open fire.

14. **Smore's Sticks:** Make your own out of sticks or get personalized sticks from Boulder and Branch. They double as hot dog or sausage sticks, too.

15. **Leather grilling gloves:** For any type of outdoor cooking you'll need these.

16. **Digital thermometer:** Needed to check the temperature of meats. These come with a probe and a digital reader.

17. **Oven thermometer:** For a wood fired oven you'll need one that goes to higher temperatures than normal. Get one that goes to 750 degrees at Amazon. A laser thermometer also works well.

18. **Meat injector:** For the serious chef these allow the insertion of flavored liquids into the meat before cooking.

19. **Grill Baskets:** Place veggies in these for easing cooking on the grill or in the oven or smoker.

20. **Grill Lights:** These sit on a magnet base and stand upright. Use when cooking in the oven or on the grill in the dark.

Tips for Cooking Fish on the Grill

Grilling fish takes a bit of planning because it has a tendency to stick. If you are not using a fish basket, here are some tips to help you get through the cooking process without destroying the fish.

1. Make sure that the grill is super clean to start with. The best time to clean is when it is still hot and the food bits come of more easily.

2. If you don't have a grill brush, use a scrunched up ball of foil held with tongs.

3. Lightly oil the grate and the fish. Leave the skin on to reduce sticking. Lightly apply salt and pepper. Cook skin side down first. Salmon works great because it is thicker and oiler that other types of fish, and will cook up nicely placed directly on the grill.

4. Grill the fish longer on the first side to allow it to create a sear. Cook with the lid closed to allow the second side to begin cooking as well.

5. Alternatively, use a cedar plank. Season with salt and pepper, and place lemon slices on top, then place on the grill.

6. If you prefer, use a cast iron skillet or fish basket.

Meat Temperature Chart

Cook meat to the internal temperatures listed below. Use a digital thermometer inserted into the center of the meat.

Type of Meat	Temp F	Temp C
Chicken	165° F	74 ° C
Turkey	165° F	74° C
Fish with tails	145° F	63° C
Beef, Veal, or Lamb Rare	125° F	55° C
Beef, Veal, or Lamb Med Rare	135° F	57° C
Beef, Veal, or Lamb Medium	145° F	71° C
Beef, Veal or Lamb Med Well	155° F	74° C
Beef, Veal or Lamb Well	160° F	77° C
Brisket, Pork Butts	205° F	96° C
Pork	145° -155°F	63° C
Ham	145° F	63° C
Pulled Pork	205° F	96° C
Ground meat: beef, veal, lamb, pork. Sausage.	160° F	71° C
Hot dogs, stuffing, casseroles	165° F	74° C

Chapter 6

Schools and Training Resources

Oven Building and Cooking Schools

Borner Farm Project
Prescott, WI
Learn to Bake in a Wood-Fired
Oven, Brick Oven Basics– Build-
ing & Baking classes. Instructor;
David S. Cargo
bornerfarmproject@gmail.com
www.bornerfarmproject.com
Call Diane at 651-235-4906 for
more info.

**Bread Bakers Guild of
America**
IBIE Lectures—Las Vegas, NV
October 9-11 2016
Adding Artisan Breads to Your
Bakery, Wheat Breeding & Practi-
cal Uses for the Baker.
www.bbga.org

Breadhitz
Rehoboth, MA
Learn to make many different
types of breads from master chef
Ciril Hitz. Offers different day
long and three-day workshops,
and some oven building classes.
www.breadhitz.com
chef@breadhitz.com

Cob Workshops
www.cobworkshops.org

Edwards & Eve Cob Building
Norfolk, England
www.cobcourses.com

**Goodfella's Pizza School of
New York**
Four-Day Pizza Class; Master of
Pizza Operations; Consulting.
Hands-on professional courses
offered weekly. 718-987-2422
www.pizzaschoolnewyork.com

International School of Pizza
San Francisco, CA
Neapolitan and classic Italian style
pizza combo and other 5-day
courses with Tony Genmignani.
internationalschoolofpizza.com
E-mail: Shana@rootedinclay.com

**Jillyanna's Woodfired Cooking
School**
Learn how to make pizza, pies,
pasta, and entire meals
Kennebunkport, Maine
207-967-4960
cook@jillyannas.com
www.jillannas.com

King Arthur Baking Education Centers
Workshops in Norwich, Vermont, and across the country. Introductory demonstrations for beginners to intensive week-long courses for the professional. Bread, croissants, gluten free, cakes, artisan baking, biscuits and scones, French tarts, flatbreads, and more for the home chef or pro.
E-mail: bakingeducation@kingarthurflour.com
800-652-3334
www.kingarthurflour.com

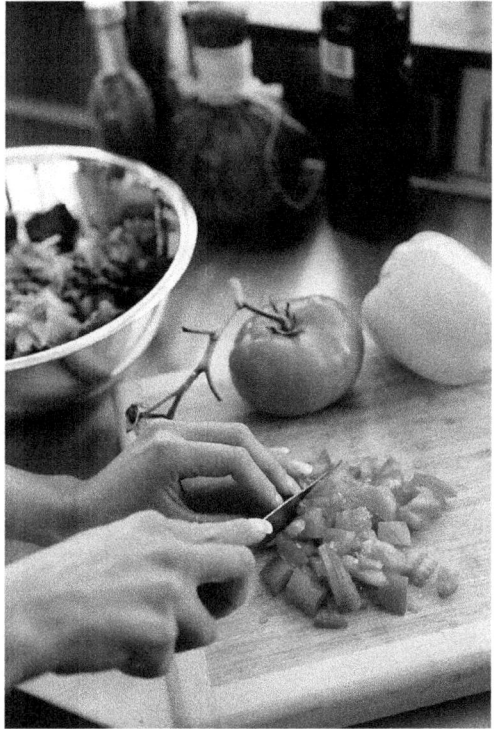

Maine Grain Alliance Workshops
Maine
Sept—October, 2016
The BIG Bake at the Common Ground Country Fair, and Leavening Workshop Oct 16-18.
www.kneadingconference.com

Manna from Devon Cooking School and B&B
Devon, England
Offers Wood-Fired Oven 1—Mastering Your Oven, Wood-Fired Oven 2– Baking and Slow Cooking, Private Woodfired Oven Classes and a Bed and Breakfast.

Phone: 01803 752943
www.mannafromdevon.com

Masonry Heater Association of North America
Wood-fired oven and masonry heater workshops at various locations throughout the U.S. and Canada by Certified Heater Masons. Contact Richard Smith, Executive Director
Visit www.mha-net.org for more information.

Mugniani Cooking School
1—7 day classes
Watsonville, CA; Healdsburg, CA; Tuscany, Italy

www.mugniaini.com
888-887-7206

North House Folk School
Grand Marais, Minnesota
Ovencrafting: Building and Baking
in the Wood-Fired Brick Oven (4
days), also baking classes and other
interesting courses.
info@northhouse.org
218-387-9762
www.northhouse.org

**Portable Brick Oven Classes
with David S. Cargo**
Various locations
spbc.info/quest/portable-
classes.html

**Pizza Cooking Class in Chianti
Program**
Chianti, Italy
Learn to make pizza with a Naples
native. Secretes and recipes of real
Italian pizza, then enjoy your piz-
za .2.5 hours
www.lebaccanti.com

Rolling Fire
Seattle, Washington
Hands-on cooking classes: Italian
pizza and managing the fire.
www.rollingfire.com
206-659-7699
mike@rollingfire.com

Rooted in Clay
Rindge, New Hampshire
Introduction to Cob Building and
Wood-fired Ovens
www.rootedinclay.com
E-mail: Shana@rootedinclay.com
603-899-3120

Stone Turtle Baking Center
Cooking classes using a wood-
fired oven. All skill levels.
Lyman, ME
207-459-0567
info@stoneturtlebaking.com
www.stoneturtlebaking.com

**Sun Dog School of Natural
Building**
Learn how to build rocket mass
heaters and other things out of
cob.
http://www.sundogbuilders.net/

The Borgo Cooking School
Palazetto, Italy
Learn to make perfect Italian pizzas and breads in a traditional
open-air wood burning oven. Les-
sons are in Italian with an English
interpreter.
Phone: +39 0577 75 1222
www.borgocookingschool.com
E-mail:
info@borgosantopietro.com

The Fresh Loaf
Dallas, Texas
Wood-fired oven artisan bread cooking class and pizza cooking class.
Phone: 469-484-4990
www.bredstoneovens.com
info@breadstoneovens.com

The School of Artisan Food
Nottinghamshire, England
Short and long courses on advanced bread baking, pizza making and more.
Phone: 01909 532171
info@schoolofartisanfood.org
www.schoolofartisanfood.org

Wood-Fired Cooking
With Mary Karlin
Private hands-on wood-fired cooking classes
Northern California
mary4cheese@gmail.com
www.wood-firedcooking.com

Wildwood Ovens Test Kitchen Cooking Classes
Learn how to cook in a wood-fired oven and Brazilian BBQ.
Los Angeles, CA
323-255-6578
info@wildwoodovens.com
www.losangelescookingclasses.net

Brick Pizza Oven Building Workshops
Downloadable
By Rado Hand
Australia
www.traditionaloven.com

Resources for Wood-Fired Heating

Chimney Safety Institute of America
2155 Commercial Drive, Plainfield, IN 46168
(317) 837-5362 Fax: (317) 837-5365
E-Mail: office@csia.org
Website: csia.org
The CSIA is an educational organization and operates out of the CSIA Technology Center. Find a CSIA Certified Chimney Sweep here.

Masonry Heater Association of North America
Richard (Dick) Smith, Administrator
execdir@mha-net.org
www.mha-net.org
520-883-0191
Find a Certified Heater Mason here.

National Fireplace Institute
1601 North Kent Street, Suite 1001
Arlington, VA 22209 USA
Phone: 703/524-8030 Fax: 703/522-0548

Email: info@nficertified.org
Website: www.nficertified.org
Find a NFI Certified professional here. Current certifications offered are *Woodburning Specialist, Gas Specialist, Pellet Specialist* and *Master Hearth Professional.*

Bellfires Fireplaces
www.bellfiresusa.com
Find a dealer/installer here

Rumford Fireplaces
www.rumford.com
Find a Rumford mason here

Good Time Stove Company
188 Cape St Rt 112
Gopshen, MA
416-268-3677
www.goodtimestove.com
A large collection of antique cast iron stoves and Franklin fireplaces circa 1840—1930 is on display at this location. The company specializes in refurbishing old stoves.

Environmental Protection Agency
www.epa.gov
The EPA Certifies wood-burning appliances.

Consumer Product Safety Commission. www.cpsc.gov
Check recalls on equipment and appliances.

www.Hearth.com: A comprehensive site with lots of information for homeowners and chimney professionals alike.

www.chimneysweeps.com
Lots of information and articles for homeowners.

Best Home Gear
https://besthomegear.com/how-much-is-a-cord-of-wood-and-other-firewood-facts-you-can-use

CO Headquarters
Dr. David Penny has created a website with much information about Carbon Monoxide
www.coheadquarters.com

Codes and Standards

ASTM International (American Society for Testing and Materials)
610-832-9585
E-mail: service@astm.org
www.astm.org
Formerly the *American Society for Testing and Materials*, is an international standards organization that develops and publishes voluntary consensus technical standards for a wide range of materials, products, systems, and services including clay flue liners, bricks, clay flue lining methods, and more.

ANSI (American National Standards Institute)
1819 L Street, NW
Suite 600
Washington, DC 20036
(202) 293-8020
The Institute oversees the creation, promulgation and use of thousands of norms and guidelines that directly impact businesses in nearly every sector: from acoustical devices to construction equipment, from dairy and livestock production to energy distribution, and many more.

ICC (International Code Council)
1-888-422-7233
www.iccsafe.org

Writes the International Residential Code. You may purchase the IRC online in disk format and print as necessary or view as a PDF file. As of the time of publication of this book the IRC has been accepted by most jurisdictions in the United States, however, some fire marshals follow the NFPA Standard, so it would be prudent to follow the more restrictive requirements of the two publications. The codes are proposed by building officials only, and new proposals are not currently being accepted by outside sources. Also be careful to check your local building code officials, which may alter the IRC in their city. Also publishes the international Fuel Gas Code

NFPA (National Fire Protection Association)
800 -344-3555

E-mail: customerservice@nfpa.org

www.nfpa.org

You may purchase the latest edition of the NFPA 211 Standard from this website.

(NFPA writes the NFPA 211 Standard for Chimneys, Fireplaces, Vents, and Solid Fuel-Burning Appliances) This is a Standard, not a code — unless adopted by city code. It is the Standard that has been used in our industry for many years. Fire marshals may still use this standard even if the code official does not.

CCBFC Canadian Commission on Building and Fire Codes

(613) 993-9960

www.nationalcodes.ca

The Canadian Commission on Building and Fire Codes (CCBFC) develops and maintains six of Canada's model construction and fire codes and oversees the work of several standing committees, special purpose committees, and task groups. CCBFC members are selected from across Canada and appointed by the National Research Council (NRC).

Suggested Reading

British Chimney Sweeps: Five Centuries of Chimney Sweeping
by Benita Cullingford
(Paperback - May 25, 2001)

Jay Shelton's Solid Fuel Encyclopedia
By Jay Shelton
(Dec 1982)

Wood Heat Safety
By Jay Shelton
(Dec 1979)

Fire Places: A Practical Design Guide to Fireplaces and Stoves Indoors and Out
by Jane Gitlin
(Paperback - Nov 21, 2006)

Fireplaces, Chimneys & Stoves
by Michael Waumsley
(Hardcover - Aug 1, 2005)

The Fireplace Book
By Miranda Innes
(Hardcover—Nov 2, 2000)
Fireplace design ideas.

Fireplace Book II
An Idea Book of Fireplace Designs
Aberdeen's Magazine of Masonry Construction (Dec 1995)

What's in Style: Fireplaces
By Joanne Still (Paperback—Aug 2002)
Fireplace design ideas.

Masonry Fireplace and Chimney Handbook
By James E Amhrein
(Paperback June, 1995)

The Forgotten Art of Building a Good Fireplace
By Vrest Orton
(Paperback—March 22, 2005)
How to alter unsatisfactory fireplaces and build new ones in the Rumford fashion)

Building A Fireplace: Step-by-step Instructions For Contemporary To Classic Styles (Schiffer Books)
By Bernd Grutzmacher

(Paperback Aug 30, 2004)
Masonry Skills
Richard T Kreh
(Paperback, 1997)

The Book of Masonry Stoves
Rediscovering a New Way of
Warming
By David Lyle

From the Wood-Fired Oven:
New and Traditional
Techniques for Cooking and
Baking with Fire
by Richard Miscovich

Build Your Own Barrel Oven:
A Guide for making a versatile,
efficient, and easy to use wood-
fired oven
By Max and Eva Edleson
(Paperback - 2012)

Rocket Mass Heaters: Third
Edition
By Ianto Evans and Leslie Jackson
(Paperback - 2014)
The "Bible" of Rocket Mass
heaters.

References

The Forgotten Art of Fireplace Building by Vrest Orton

Rocket Mass Heaters Third Edition by Ianto Evans and Leslie Jackson, Cobb Cottage Company, 2014

Harbison Walker International Pocket Reference Guide

The Woodburner's Companion: Practical Ways of Heating with Wood by Dirk Thomas, Alan Hood and Company, 2000

Build Your Own Barrel Oven by Max and Eva Edelson, Hand Print Press 2012

HearthMasters, Inc.: www.chimkc.com

The Chimney and Hearth Pro's Resource Book by Marge Padgitt, HearthMasters Publishing 2021

Wikipedia.org

Traditional Oven: By Rado Hand https://www.traditionaloven.co

Ahren Fire Fireplaces (http://ahrenfire.com)

Bellfires Fireplaces (https://bellfiresusa.com)

ECCO Stove: www.eccostove.com

Archguard Fireplace/masonry heater: www.archguard.com

Rocket Stove Books: https://www.rocketstoves.com

Cozy Grate Heater: www.thermo-rite.com

HeatShield PriorFire Retrofit Fireplace System: https://heatshieldchimney.com/priorfire/

WoodMaster Furnaces: https://www.woodmaster.com/product-category/cleanfire-outdoor-wood-furnaces/

Carbon Monoxide Headquarters: Dr. David Penney www.coheadquarters.com

Join these Facebook Groups:

Wood-Fired Ovens/Barbecues/Smokers

Masonry Heater/Rocket Heaters/Kachelofen Hub

Facebook Pages:

HearthMasters, Inc.
HearthMasters Publishing

Read our Blogs:

Wood-Fired Heating and Cooking
woodfiredheatingandcooking.blogspot.com

HearthMasters

About the Authors

Gene Padgitt

Gene is a veteran chimney technician, chimney sweep, expert mason, and fire investigator.

He is the vice president of HearthMasters, Inc. and Padgitt Forensic Investigations in Kansas City, Missouri. Gene specializes in masonry heater, brick oven, chimney, and fireplace construction with brick or stone, and diagnosing problems with gas and wood-fired appliances.

Padgitt is a Missouri State Certified Private Fire Investigator, CSIA Certified Chimney Sweep, NFI Certified Gas Technician, Certified Heater Mason, and has a degree in HVACR Technology. He studied photography at the Kansas City Art Institute.

Gene investigates structural fires related to chimneys and heating appliances and serves as an expert witness for court cases. To date, he has completed over 300 fire investigations and over 60,000 chimney/fireplace inspections.

He has co-authored books and articles, and has taught numerous classes for trade organizations such as the National Chimney Sweep Guild, the Midwest Chimney Safety Council, and for HearthMasters, Inc. Masonry School. Gene served on the board of directors for the MCSC for 20 years.

Gene and Marge also own a real estate investment company and enjoy restoring older homes. Gene has been accused of being one of "those guys" who know how to do almost anything, but don't tell anyone.

Contact Gene at www.chimkc.com.

Marge Padgitt

Marge joined Gene in the chimney business in 1985. She is a CSIA Certified Chimney Sweep, NFI Certified Woodburning Specialist and trainer, and is a Missouri State Licensed Private Investigator.

Marge is the president of HearthMasters, Inc. and Padgitt Forensic Investigations. She served on the board of directors for the National Chimney Sweep Guild, the Midwest Hearth, Patio, and Barbecue Association, and the Masonry Heater Association of North America.

Padgitt served on the board of directors of the Midwest Chimney Safety Council from 1993 to 2019, and was president, newsletter editor, magazine editor, and served as webmaster for the association.

Marge has spoken at over 150 meetings and conferences, and has created multiple presentations about business building, marketing, contracts, and technical applications.

Marge has written over 250 articles for examiner.com, chimneys.com, SNEWS Magazine, SWEEPING, Magazine, Masonry Construction Magazine, her blog Wood-Fired Heating and Cooking and other publications. She is the author of The Chimney and Hearth Pro's Resource Book, The Lombardo Family History and Cookbook, and 14 books in different genres. Marge operates HearthMasters Publishing Company and publishes books by other authors as well as her own.

She is a classical and jazz musician (bass), and studied music, theatre, and business at CMSU, UMKC, and UMC. She is also one of the family genealogists.

Marge and Gene live in Kansas City Missouri with their cat, Patches.

Contact Marge at www.chimkc.com or office@chimkc.com.

Publications by HearthMasters, Inc.

Wood-Fired Magazine
Editor-in-Chief Marge Padgitt
www.lulu.com

The Chimney and Hearth Pro's Resource Book
by Marge Padgitt
www.amazon.com

Presentations for Chimney & Hearth Professionals
By Marge Padgitt
5-CD Set

Wood-Fired Heating and Cooking
By Gene and Marge Padgitt

Coming soon:

Inspecting Chimneys and Fireplaces
By Gene and Marge Padgitt

Investigating Structural Fires Related to Chimneys and Heating Appliances For Fire Investigators
By Gene and Marge Padgitt

The Complete Guide to Chimney and Fireplace Restoration
By Gene and Marge Padgitt

See a complete list of publications at www.hearthmasters.net

Wood-Fired